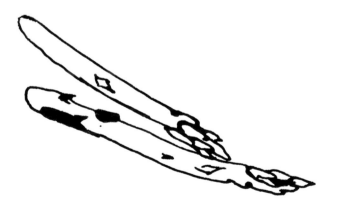

*Photography:* Charlie Drevstam
*Illustrations:* Stina Wirsén

# Tina Nordström's Weekend Cooking

## Old & New Recipes for Your Fridays, Saturdays, and Sundays

## Tina Nordström

### Translated by Gun Penhoat

Skyhorse Publishing

# CONTENTS

# IT'S THE WEEKEND, FINALLY!

As the child of tavern owners, I wasn't exactly spoiled by endless family weekend get-togethers. Weekends were when my parents' restaurant was busiest, so our days off were just as likely to fall on a Wednesday as any other weekday.

Now as an adult, I consider the weekend—Friday, Saturday, and Sunday—to be a mini-vacation, so no matter where I am in the world, I do my best to make my way home and spend time with my family.

The weekend is important, not only because it marks the end of the workweek, but because it allows us to enjoy family life and recharge our batteries for the week ahead. Food plays a critical role here.

A good meal is about much more than the food itself—it's about the experience. Careful consideration and planning is required when we're deciding on where,

how, and with whom to eat. All these factors are just as important as what we eat.

And don't forget to include the kids! Have dinner at 3 p.m. if they're too young to stay up later in the evening. Set the table with nicely folded napkins, and make time for a pre-dinner drink (for the grown-ups) in the living room before sitting down to eat. This doesn't require you to go fancy every day; a simple meal is fine, too, and can be every bit as enjoyable as an elaborate dinner.

I like to dust off old ideas and recipes that have had time to mature over the years and update them. The prettily adorned sandwich cake, the hot sandwich, the baked potato—I think all of them deserve a second look.

*Tina*

# Pairing Food and Drink

*The expression "birds of a feather" even applies to what's on the dinner table, which is why your choice of beverage should complement the food.*

*Sommeliers or wine connoisseurs can help you match a wine's body, levels of acidity, sweetness, dryness, bitterness, and barrel characteristics to any dish you want to make. Still, consider the pairings a suggestion and not a rule, since what pleases your palate will ultimately be the correct choice. My hope is that you will venture out and try a variety of combinations, while keeping in mind the advice contained within these pages. There will be times when you come upon that amazing match of food and drink where, suddenly, the more you get to experience this magic, the better.*

Begin by figuring out what flavor is dominant on your plate (it rarely turns out to be the fish or meat). Then select a drink that complements that particular flavor.

Perhaps you will choose a wine from the same region as the food you're serving; for example, what would people drink in Mexico? Here you'll need to find out what works well with Mexican food. Along those same lines, you'll find delectable truffles in northern Italy, where there is a long tradition of cultivating vineyards, making it more than likely that this area will produce many northern Italian wines that pair naturally with that delicate mushroom.

WINE

Try to reflect the meal's flavors in your choice of wine. If your dish is acidic, white wine with notes of citrus (or perhaps some sparkling water garnished with a wedge of lime) would be good. If a red wine calls to mind black currants, a dollop of black currant jelly with the food will enhance that pairing. Or, why not even add a splash of this wine to the sauce?

To complement a meal featuring a rich Béarnaise sauce, it makes sense to look for a fuller-bodied wine, since the food's high fat content will blunt the taste of the wine; this way you'll get to enjoy the wine as much as the food. Wine that is on the sweet side will temper heat and bring out the flavors in a dish, which is why it's a good idea to drink a sweeter white wine when eating food containing a lot of chili pepper.

If a wine is too dry, try adding more salt to the food—this will smooth over the roughness of the wine.

And finally, wines served with dessert should always taste sweeter than the dessert itself, as this allows them to fully come into their own.

## The Five Basic Tastes

SOUR. In food, acidic ingredients curb a beverage's sourness, smooth out roughness, and bring out fruity and sweet notes.

SALT in food decreases dryness and enhances fruity flavors and sweetness in drinks.

BITTER ingredients in food heighten a beverage's bitter taste, so it's best to avoid hoppy beer and wine aged in oak barrels when eating bitter foods.

SWEET in food cuts down on the fruitiness and sweetness of a beverage while bringing out sour and bitter tastes.

UMAMI (a savory taste—think egg or fish sauces) pulls out the metallic taste in drinks, so avoid very dry and bitter beverages (oak barrel–aged red wines, for example) and select fruitier options instead.

## How Do I Choose?

Rich and flavorful dish = fruity and full-bodied beverage

•

Dish with high acidity = high acidity in beverage

•

Light food = delicate beverage.

•

Rich desserts = fortified dessert wine (marsala, port)

•

Light desserts = delicate dessert wine (Muscat, Sauternes)

# Beer, Sparkling Wine, and Other Delights

*A keen interest in beer has blossomed in recent years, so now many more varieties exist. You can even buy alcohol-free beer, and these days you can also find good alcohol-free wines or wines with low alcohol content.*

### BEER

Naturally, the taste rules we outlined on the preceding page also apply to beer; keep an eye out for acidity, bitterness, and sweetness. Generally speaking, lagers are lighter and less bitter than ales, dark beers, and pale ales. Why not try the German Weissbier, a flavorful wheat beer? It's slightly bitter, naturally acidic, and pairs well with most foods, but is especially nice with fish and Asian cuisine.

### SPARKLING WINE

Sparkling beverages make excellent party drinks. They're often light and fresh, with sharp acidity and good carbonation, and are therefore a great match for seafood and more delicate fish dishes. The popular Italian Prosecco, slightly fruitier and more flowery than its French counterparts, Champagne and Crémant, is an excellent budget-friendly option. The Spanish Cava is another great choice.

### ALCOHOL-FREE

An influx of new and exciting alcohol-free options has appeared on store shelves these past few years—everything from wine, cider, and beer to interesting drinks produced by local manufacturers. For example, a flavorful and well-made Swedish apple juice with fresh acidity is a great alternative to white wine and can be enjoyed by children as well as adults who prefer to go alcohol free. A few Swedish classics such as lingonberry or black currant squash (syrups made from fruit concentrate and sugar) are nice and fruity alternatives to lighter red wines.

### PLAIN OLD WATER

Don't forget to set the table with water glasses, too! Plain water is just fine, but if you want to dress it up a bit, add in slices of cucumber, lemon, lime, or some other fruit. Why not try some freshly sliced ginger?

# A fresh drink and some snacks . . .

*. . . are what's needed to keep guests happy—and to quell hunger pangs while you're putting the finishing touches in the kitchen. Instead of relying on Coca-Cola or other soft drinks out of sheer habit, why not serve the kids an alcohol-free beverage? Of course, you can buy bags of roasted nuts at the grocery store, but making your own can also be fun. These snacks will be gone in the blink of an eye.*

## Cucumber Drink with Parsley and Lime

SERVES 4

*2 cucumbers, peeled*
*2 bunches (each 1 oz./30 g) fresh parsley*
*2½ cups (6 dl) sparkling water*
*1 tbsp honey*
*juice of 3 limes*
*ice cubes*

DIRECTIONS:

1. Cut the cucumber into chunks. Blend the cucumber and parsley thoroughly with an immersion blender. Add the mixture to water, honey, and lime juice in a pitcher.
2. Add the ice cubes, and serve the drink chilled.

## Watermelon Shake

SERVES 4

*1 (4½ oz./125 g) container red currants*
*4 cups (1 liter/10 dl) peeled watermelon, peeled, cubed*
*12 ice cubes*
*2 cups (½ liter/5 dl) lemonade or soda water*

DIRECTIONS :

1. Place 4 glasses in the freezer.
2. Blend red currants, melon, ice cubes, and lemonade or soda water. Pour into a pitcher and place in the refrigerator.
3. Serve the drink in ice-cold glasses.

## Green Iced Tea with Mint

SERVES 4

*8 cups (2 liters/20 dl) water*
*8 bags green tea*
*1 bunch fresh mint + 2 sprigs for garnish*
*½ cup (1 dl) superfine granulated sugar*
*¼–⅓ cup (½–¾ dl) lime juice, freshly squeezed (approx. 4 limes)*
*2 cups (½ liter/5 dl) ice cubes*
*1 lime, cut into wedges*

DIRECTIONS:

1. Bring the water to a boil. Drop the teabags in the water and let them steep together with some sprigs of mint for several minutes.
2. Add the sugar and stir until it has dissolved completely. Strain the tea and let it cool.
3. Add the lime juice. Put the ice cubes into a pitcher, and add the tea. Garnish with sprigs of mint and lime wedges. Serve the tea chilled.

# Granola Nuts with Cinnamon and Poppy Seeds

SERVES 4

*¾ cup (2 dl) rolled oats*
*3 tbsp poppy seeds*
*¼ cup (½ dl) coconut flakes*
*¼ cup (½ dl) brown sugar*
*1 tsp ground cinnamon*
*½ tsp salt*
*1 egg white*
*1–2 tbsp apple juice*
*2½ cups (6 dl) walnuts, pecans, or hazelnuts*

DIRECTIONS:

1. Preheat the oven to 340°F (170°C). Line a baking sheet with parchment paper.
2. In a food processor, place the oats, poppy seeds, coconut flakes, sugar, cinnamon, and salt and pulse using a few short bursts to mix them. (DO NOT grind to a powder.)
3. In a bowl, lightly stir or whisk the egg white and apple juice together with a fork. Fold the nuts and then the granola mixture into the egg white until the nuts are coated.
4. Spread the nut mixture onto the prepared baking sheet. Roast the mixture for 20 to 25 minutes, until the nuts are crisp and golden brown. Stir the mixture a few times while roasting. Let the mix cool on the baking sheet.

# Walnuts Roasted in Butter and Rosemary

SERVES 4

*2 tsp butter*
*2 tsp fresh rosemary, chopped*
*2 cups (5 dl) walnuts*
*1 tsp sea salt*
*black pepper, freshly ground*

DIRECTIONS:

1. Preheat the oven to 300°F (150°C). Line a baking sheet with parchment paper.
2. Melt the butter and rosemary together. Mix in the walnuts and add the sea salt and some freshly ground black pepper.
3. Place the nuts on the prepared baking sheet and roast them for approximately 30 minutes. Let them cool on the baking sheet.

# Almonds, Pine Nuts, and Seeds Roasted in Maple Syrup

SERVES 4

*2 cups (5 dl) sweet almonds*
*¾ cup (2 dl) pine nuts*
*1¼ cups (3 dl) pumpkin seeds*
*¾ cup (2 dl) watermelon seeds*
*2–3 tbsp maple syrup*
*1 tbsp cold-pressed canola oil*
*1 tsp hot paprika powder*
*1 tsp salt*

DIRECTIONS:

1. Preheat the oven to 350°F (175°C).
2. Place the almonds, pine nuts, and seeds on a rimmed baking sheet lined with parchment paper. Roast for 8 to 10 minutes, or until the nuts and seeds have turned a nice golden brown color.
3. Mix together the maple syrup, oil, paprika powder, and salt. Pour over the almond/seed mixture and stir thoroughly. Continue to roast for another 10 minutes. Let cool on the baking sheet.

Friday

*Welcome!*
It's Friday—pressure's off and you're feeling good—and you don't feel like making anything too elaborate to eat. Perhaps you just want an easy meal to share with a neighbor, a happy hour snack with friends, or a little something for a cozy Friday with the family. Wrap things up with a hot toddy and see everyone doze off contentedly on a comfy couch.

3.

5.

7.

6.

8.

4.

1.

2.

# Happy Hour

*This is the grown-up way to end the workweek: invite some colleagues or friends over for some refreshments and light snacks, or stop in for happy hour at a local pub on the way home. Even if many insist on changing out of their suits before heading out for a get-together among coworkers, the appropriate way to take part in this outing is to stay in business attire—this will help keep things in the right context.*

## 1. Quick Cheese Fondue with Sourdough Bread

Wrap some aluminum foil around the wooden cheese box to prevent the cheese from spreading all over the oven as it melts—the riper the cheese, the more it will spread.

SERVES 4
*1 clove garlic*
*1¼ lb. (500 g) Vacherin Mont d'Or or Harbison*
*⅓ cup (¾ dl) dry white wine*
*sourdough bread, for serving*

DIRECTIONS:
1. Preheat the oven to 390°F (200°C).
2. Peel the garlic and slice it thinly. Make small slits in the cheese and insert the slivers of garlic into the slits. Spoon white wine over the cheese so that it gets into the slits. Place the cheese, in its aluminum foil–wrapped packaging, into the oven, and bake for 15 to 20 minutes.
3. Remove the cheese from the oven; dip some chunks of sourdough bread into the cheese and enjoy it as a quick fondue. Try serving a semidry wine such as Sauvignon Blanc or a plain beer like lager.

## 2. Soft Cheeses with Fig Compote

SERVES 4
3 SOFT DESSERT CHEESES OF YOUR CHOICE
*(I've Chosen La Tour, Langres, and Selle de Chèvre)*
FIG COMPÔTE:
*6 fresh figs*
*2–3 tbsp raw cane sugar*
*2 tbsp balsamic vinegar*
*½ cup (1 dl) sultanas or raisins*
*1 oz. (3 cl) grappa or whiskey*

DIRECTIONS:
1. Set cheeses on a platter or cutting board and let them sit at room temperature for at least 20 minutes to bring out full flavors.
2. Cut figs into small segments.
3. In a saucepan over medium heat, melt sugar until golden brown and caramelized. Add in figs and vinegar, and let simmer until sugar has dissolved and figs have softened. Stir in sultanas and grappa or whiskey, and remove pan from heat.
4. Serve the compote lukewarm with the cheese. This goes really well with a glass of port

## 3. Cheese Saganaki (Fried Cheese) with Tomato, Pomegranate, and Sumac

Sumac is an acidic spice made from small, dried berries. You can replace the sumac with finely grated lime peel.

SERVES 4

*½ lb. (250 g) each of 2 cheeses for saganaki (halloumi, kasseri, or sheep's feta, for example)*
*olive oil for frying*
*1¼ lb. (500 g) tomatoes, preferably different varieties*
*1 shallot*
*1 pomegranate*
*1½ tsp crushed sumac (can be replaced with finely grated peel of 1 lime)*
*2 tbsp olive oil*
*salt*
*black pepper, freshly ground*

DIRECTIONS:

1. In a hot skillet, fry the cheese until golden brown, approximately 2 minutes on each side.
2. Cut the tomatoes in half, and place them in a bowl. Peel and finely chop the shallot. Remove the seeds from the pomegranate.
3. Mix the shallot with the tomatoes, and add in the pomegranate seeds and sumac. Drizzle with olive oil and season with salt and freshly ground black pepper.
4. Serve immediately, along with a crisp Swedish apple juice that matches the acidity of the dish or with a beer with citrus notes.

## 4. Zucchini, Tomato, and Prosciutto Skewers with Mint and Garlic Dressing

These skewers are very tasty when cooked on an outdoor grill; if using wooden skewers, however, make sure to soak them in water beforehand or they could catch fire on the grill's hot grate.

SERVES 4

*1 medium-sized green zucchini*
*1 medium-sized yellow zucchini*
*12 slices (6 ½ oz./175 g) prosciutto or Capicola/ Coppa salami*
*1 (5 oz./150 g) jar sun-dried tomatoes in oil*

MINT AND GARLIC DRESSING:

*2 garlic cloves*
*4 tbsp fresh mint, chopped*
*4 tbsp lime juice, freshly squeezed*
*¼ cup (½ dl) olive oil*
*salt*
*black pepper, freshly ground*

DIRECTIONS:

1. Preheat the oven and the grill to 480°F (250°C).
2. Thinly slice the zucchini—this is done most easily with a kitchen mandolin.
3. Alternating the zucchini, salami, and tomatoes, thread the food onto the skewers and then place them in an ovenproof casserole.
4. Peel and crush the garlic cloves for the dressing. In a bowl, mix the crushed garlic with mint, lime juice, and olive oil. Season with salt and pepper.
5. Brush the skewers lightly with some of the dressing and grill them for about 3 to 5 minutes.
6. Place the skewers on a platter and spoon the remaining dressing over them. Serve immediately with a light and fruity red wine.

# 5. Oven-Toasted Liba Bread

Liba is the name of a Lebanese flatbread; you should be able to find it in well-stocked grocery stores.

SERVES 4

*1 package liba flatbread*
*1–2 tbsp olive oil*
*sea salt*

DIRECTIONS:

1. Preheat the oven to 390°F (200°C).
2. Brush the bread with some olive oil, sprinkle it with sea salt, and toast them in the oven until they're golden brown and crispy.
3. Serve the bread with beet and chickpea spread (recipe #6) or bean and avocado spread with cashews. (recipe #7 on following page).

# 6. Beet and Chickpea Spread

SERVES 4

*1 (14½ oz./400 g) can chickpeas*
*1–2 boiled beets (can be purchased precooked)*
*2 tbsp olive oil*
*½ lemon, grated peel and juice*
*1 tbsp tahini or 2 tbsp roasted sesame seeds*
*1 tsp ground cumin*
*salt*
*black pepper, freshly ground*

DIRECTIONS:

1. Using a food processor or an immersion blender, mix all ingredients except the salt and pepper until smooth.
2. Season with salt and freshly ground pepper.
3. Serve the spread with Lebanese (Liba) flatbread.

**WHAT TO DRINK**
To accompany the bread and spreads, try a sparkling semidry white wine—perhaps a Crémant de Bourgogne or similar beverage.

# 7. Bean and Avocado Spread with Cashews

SERVES 4

*2 avocados*
*1 (14½ oz./400 g) can large white beans*
*½ cup (1 dl) roasted cashews*
*3 tbsp olive oil*
*1 lime, grated peel and juice*
*1 garlic clove*
*salt*
*black pepper, freshly ground*

DIRECTIONS:

1. Cut the avocados in half. Remove the pits and scoop out the flesh. Using a food processor or an immersion blender, mix all ingredients, except the salt and pepper, until smooth.
2. Season with salt and pepper.
3. Serve with Lebanese (Liba) flatbread.

# 8. Hot Shrimp with Fennel and Garlic

My teeth are like cement mixers and can happily chomp down on both un-popped popcorn kernels and shrimp shells. In this recipe, I remove the shrimp heads and eat the rest—shell and all—as I can't really be bothered with the fuss of removing the shells.

SERVES 4

*1 garlic clove*
*2 tbsp olive oil*
*1 tbsp fennel seeds, crushed*
*1 tsp chili flakes*
*1¼ lb. (500 g) unpeeled shrimp*

DIRECTIONS:

1. Peel the garlic and slice it thinly. Heat oil in a skillet and the sauté the garlic, fennel seeds, and chili flakes.
2. When the skillet is very hot, add the shrimp and cook them over high heat for 1 to 2 minutes, until they are just heated through.
3. Transfer the shrimp to a platter and serve immediately.

**WHAT TO DRINK**
A German Weissbier (wheat beer) or a crisp, acidic, semidry Riesling goes very well with shrimp.

12.

9.

10.

11.

# Baked Potato

*Clad in nineties-era stonewashed jeans and fluorescent shoelaces, a younger me could often be found at Knutpunkten (in Helsingborg, Sweden), the first café to serve baked potatoes. There, I always ordered the same meal: baked potato with top sirloin strips and horseradish-flavored butter with roasted onions. Here, however, I share four fillings with you to help bring these potatoes into the twenty-first century; make them all and let everyone choose their own favorite.*

## Baked Potatoes 3 Ways

You can bake potatoes several ways, and they are delicious whichever way you choose. The skin on a baked potato should be solid, crisp, dark brown, and taut. I always like to save the skin for last, and if my kids don't eat theirs, I'll polish theirs off, too.

SERVES 4
4 BAKING POTATOES

IN THE OVEN:

1. Preheat the oven to 390°F (200°C).
2. Pierce the potatoes all over with a fork or toothpick. Wrap the potatoes in aluminum foil and bake them for about 1 hour. Use the toothpick to check for doneness.

IN THE MICROWAVE, THEN OVEN:

1. Pierce the potatoes all over and microwave them on full power for 12 to 15 minutes, depending on the size of the potatoes.
2. Meanwhile, heat the oven to 390°F (200°C).
3. Bake the potatoes in the oven for 10 minutes to give them a nicely crisp skin.

ON THE STOVETOP, THEN THE OVEN:

1. Heat the oven to 390°F (200°C).
2. Boil the potatoes in salted water for about 30 minutes.
3. Wrap the potatoes in aluminum foil and finish baking them in the oven for approximately 15 minutes.

## 9. Baked Potato with Shrimp, Zucchini, and Soft Yolk Egg

SERVES 4

*4 eggs*
*1 red onion*
*1 zucchini*
*1½ tsp olive oil*
*½ lemon, grated peel and juice*
*salt*
*black pepper, freshly ground*
*4 baked potatoes (see preceding recipes)*
*12½ oz. (350 g) shrimp, cooked and peeled*
*1–2 tbsp butter, softened*

DIRECTIONS:

1. Place the eggs in a saucepan and cover with cold water. Bring water to a boil and set a timer for 3 minutes. When time is up, drain the water and rinse the eggs under cold water.
2. Peel the onion. Grate zucchini and onion on the coarse side of a box grater. Transfer the grated mixture in a bowl. Mix in olive oil, lemon juice, and grated peel. Season with salt and pepper.
3. Cut an X into each potato and give the potatoes a squeeze to open cuts. Place the grated zucchini salad into the openings and top with shrimp and a warm, soft-boiled egg. Add a pat of butter on top.

## 10. Baked Potato with Top Sirloin, Bell Pepper Crème, and Parsley Salad

SERVES 4

4 baked potatoes (see opposite page)
10½–14 oz. (300–400 g) roast top sirloin, kept in
   one piece
1 bunch (approx. 1 oz./30 g) parsley
¾ cup (2 dl) roasted onion, plus some for garnish
lettuce leaves (endive or romaine)

BELL PEPPER CRÈME:

1 (14½ oz./400 g) can large white beans
½ cup (1 dl) cashews
2 pickled red bell peppers from a jar (approx. 6
   oz./170 g)
juice from ½ lime
Tabasco sauce, to taste

DIRECTIONS:

1. Cube the top sirloin.
2. Chop up the parsley and mix it with the roasted onion. Tear the lettuce into bits and mix it with the parsley and onion.
3. In a food processor or with an immersion blender, blend the beans, cashews, peppers, and lime juice. Add Tabasco sauce to taste. The sauce should become red and creamy.
4. Cut an X into each potato and give them a squeeze to open cuts. Place a bit of salad into the opening and then a hearty dollop of pepper crème on top. Top it all with the sirloin cubes and roasted onion.

## 11. Baked Potato with Deluxe Cheeses, Walnuts, and Celery and Dill Salad

SERVES 4

4 baked potatoes (see opposite page)
¾ cup (2 dl) walnuts + ½ tsp salt, for roasting
2 bags (4½ oz./125 g each) mozzarella
3½–5 ¼ oz. (100–150g) Roquefort

CELERY AND DILL SALAD:

2 stalks celery
1 bunch (approx. 1 oz./30 g) dill
juice of ½ lemon
2 tbsp olive oil
salt
black pepper, freshly ground

DIRECTIONS:

1. Roast walnuts with salt in a dry skillet over medium heat until they are golden brown. Give the pan an occasional shake.
2. Chop the celery stalks on the bias. Chop the dill coarsely. Mix celery and dill with the lemon juice and olive oil. Season with salt and black pepper.
3. Cut an X into each potato and squeeze them so that the cut opens. Crumble the cheeses into the opening and let them melt together. Add the salad and top with walnuts.

**WHAT TO DRINK**
A pilsner-type beer is tasty with baked potatoes. Why not enjoy a Swedish lager or a Mexican corn beer?

## 12. Baked Potato with Ground Lamb, Avocado, and Grapefruit

These taste like tacos, but potatoes serve as the taco shells. A true, down-home Friday treat!

SERVES 4

*4 baked potatoes (see p. 26)*
*2 garlic cloves*
*1¼ lb. ground lamb*
*1 tbsp olive oil*
*1 tsp dried Mexican oregano*
*3 tsp ground cumin*
*2 tsp paprika*
*1 tsp salt*
*Tabasco, to taste (optional)*
*1 ruby red grapefruit*
*2 avocados*
*1¼ cup (3 dl) sour cream*
*1 bunch fresh cilantro*
*black pepper, freshly ground*

DIRECTIONS:

1. Peel and finely chop the garlic cloves. In a skillet, add olive oil and brown the ground lamb with garlic, spices, and salt. Make sure the ground meat is broken into fine chunks. If you want more spice in the dish, add in a few drops of Tabasco.
2. Pull the grapefruit into pith-free segments. Cut the avocados in half; remove pits and scoop out the flesh in chunks. Transfer all to a bowl.
3. Cut an X into each potato and squeeze them to open cuts. Place a generous amount of ground mix into the opening and add a dollop of sour cream. Top it all with avocado, grapefruit, and cilantro. Grind some black pepper over the top, and it's good to go!

## 13. Baked Celery Root (Celeriac) and Rutabaga

Alternate between baked potatoes and baked celery root or rutabaga to serve with a variety of delicatessen meats—they're absolutely delicious with a big pat of butter and a sprinkle of sea salt flakes. If you don't have a microwave, just bake the root vegetable in a 390°F (200°C) oven for approximately 1 hour. Wrap the vegetable in aluminum foil along with 1 tablespoon of butter or oil if cooking it in a conventional oven.

SERVES 4

*1 celery root or rutabaga*
   *(approx. 1½–1¾ lb./600–800g)*
*2 tbsp butter*
*sea salt*

DIRECTIONS:

1. Scrub and wash the root vegetable with cold water. Pierce it all over with a fork or a toothpick.
2. In the microwave, cook the whole vegetable on the highest setting for 10 to 12 minutes. Remove the vegetable, rotate it, and cook for another 10 minutes—cooking time will depend somewhat on the weight of the tuber and on how fibrous it is. Check the celery root or the rutabaga's doneness with a toothpick. The vegetable is done when it is soft straight through.
3. Place the vegetable on a platter, cut an X on the top, and dab a pat of butter in the opening. Top it with some sea salt.

**WHAT TO DRINK**
A Portuguese full-bodied, slightly sweet red wine pairs very well with these root vegetables.

13.

16.

15.

14.

17.

# Hot Sandwiches

*A hot sandwich is way up there on my list of favorite foods. At its most basic, it's a slice of white bread with smoked ham, spicy mustard, and a slice of tomato—with lots of cheese piled on. Yet, a hot sandwich can be so much more: all you need is some good sourdough bread, some salmon or prosciutto, a jar of artichoke hearts, Dijon mustard, an aromatic fresh herb, and you're good to go. Here are my current favorite sandwiches:*

## 14. Pears with Cream Cheese, Peanut Butter, and Rosemary

Since pears and honey are both very sweet, a semi-dry or maybe an alcohol-free Swedish cider made from pear or apple would pair nicely.

SERVES 2

>4 slices sourdough bread
>2 tbsp cream cheese (Philadelphia style)
>2 tbsp peanut butter
>1 pear, tart and firm
>1 lemon
>1 sprig of rosemary
>salt
>black pepper, freshly ground

DIRECTIONS:

1. Spread a generous tablespoon of cream cheese on one side of both slices of sourdough. Add a layer of peanut butter on top.
2. Peel the pear and slice it thinly. Spread the pear slices on top of the cream cheese and peanut butter layers. Squeeze some lemon juice over them. Season with salt and pepper. Sprinkle with rosemary leaves, and place the other two slices on top.
3. Grill the sandwiches in a sandwich press for 5 to 7 minutes. Serve immediately, along with a semidry or non-alcoholic Swedish apple or pear cider, and maybe some slices of tasty, smoked salami-style sausage.

## 15. Smoked Salmon with Egg and Parmesan

Smoked salmon and Parmesan have assertive flavors, so the best choice of drink here would be a nice lager with a touch of citrus.

SERVES 2

>4 slices sourdough bread
>butter or cream cheese (Philadelphia style)
>4 slices smoked salmon
>2 eggs
>1 handful baby spinach leaves
>1 bunch (approx. 1 oz./30 g) chives
>¼ cup (30 g) Parmesan, grated
>salt
>black pepper, freshly ground

DIRECTIONS:

1. Spread butter or cream cheese onto the slices of bread. Make an indentation in the middle of two of the slices (it doesn't matter if it makes a hole). Place the spinach leaves into the dent, and crack an egg over the spinach—the indentation will prevent the egg from running all over the entire slice of bread.
2. Place the salmon on the egg, and add the rest of the spinach. Snip the chives and sprinkle them and the Parmesan over the spinach. Season with salt and pepper, and top with the other two slices of bread.
3. Grill in a sandwich press for 5 to 7 minutes. Serve immediately.

## 16. Bacon, Turkey, Dijon Mayonnaise, and Cheddar Cheese

A lovely, hop-rich American ale tastes great with bacon and cheese.

SERVES 2

   *4 slices sourdough bread*
   *1 tbsp mayonnaise*
   *1 tbsp Dijon mustard*
   *4 slices smoked turkey*
   *1 pickled cucumber*
   *1 beefsteak tomato*
   *¼ cup (½ dl) cheddar or other full-fat cheese,*
      *grated*
   *black pepper, freshly ground*
   *1 bunch (approx. 1 oz./30 g) Italian parsley*
   *4 slices bacon*

DIRECTIONS:

1. Mix mayonnaise and mustard; spread onto the slices of the bread. Place the sliced turkey on two of the bread slices.
2. Slice the cucumber lengthwise, and slice the tomato. Spread the cucumber onto the turkey, and then add the tomato. Top with grated cheese and add some freshly ground black pepper. Set the other two slices of bread on top to complete the sandwiches. Place whole sprigs of parsley on top of the sandwiches and wrap each sandwich in a slice of bacon.
3. Grill in a sandwich press for about 7 minutes. Serve hot, right off the grill.

## 17. Brie, Salami, and Artichoke Hearts

The drink to enjoy here is a fruity Italian red wine, like Valpolicella.

SERVES 2

   *4 slices sourdough bread*
   *butter or cream cheese, for spreading*
      *(Philadelphia style)*
   *1 tbsp sweet, coarse-grain mustard*
   *1 (14½ oz./400 g) can artichoke hearts*
   *4 slices salami*
   *5¼ oz. (150 g) Brie*
   *honey*
   *salt*
   *black pepper, freshly ground*

DIRECTIONS:

1. Spread the slices of bread with butter or cream cheese, then add a dollop of mustard to two of the slices.
2. Cut four artichoke hearts in half. Add the slices of salami and artichokes to the slices of bread smeared with mustard.
3. Break the cheese into two chunks, then break each piece of cheese into smaller bits. Wedge small pieces of cheese between the salami and artichoke hearts. Drizzle with honey, and season with salt and pepper. Place the other slices of bread on top to complete the sandwiches.
4. Grill in a sandwich press for about 7 minutes. Serve immediately.

# 18. Prawns in Miso Bouillon

*When you buy prawns, always make sure you choose sustainably harvested varieties.*

### SERVES 4

2 parsley roots
1 carrot
3 garlic cloves
1 stalk lemongrass
2-inch (5 cm) piece fresh ginger
1 bok choy
oil, for frying
3 tbsp miso paste
2 tsp rice vinegar
4 cups (1 liter/10 dl) water
5¼ oz. (150 g) cellophane noodles
½ lb. (250 g) of prawns, peeled
butter, for frying

### DIRECTIONS:

1. Peel and slice parsley roots and carrot into coins. Peel the garlic cloves and crush them with the side of a knife blade. Slice the lemongrass into thin strips. Peel and finely chop the ginger. Cut the bok choy into chunks.

2. In a saucepan, sauté parsley roots, carrot, garlic, lemongrass, and ginger in a little bit of oil.

3. Add in the miso paste, rice vinegar, and water. Bring to a boil, and let simmer for 5 minutes.

4. Add in the noodles and the bok choy, and let everything simmer for a few more minutes.

5. In a skillet, quickly sauté the prawns with some butter and oil. Season with salt and pepper. Stir the prawns into the bouillon, and dig in!

**WHAT TO DRINK**

Sweet and sour are the dominant flavors in this Asian noodle soup, so pair it with a young, crisp Riesling or a tart wheat beer—both go very well with eastern cuisine!

# 19. Steak Salad with Dinosaur Kale and Sesame Seeds

*Dinosaur kale, also known as palm tree kale, is a cross between kale and savoy cabbage. It is reminiscent of spinach but has a more pronounced flavor. If you can't find dinosaur kale, it's okay to use savoy cabbage instead.*

**SERVES 4**

1½–1¾ lb. (600–800 g) sirloin steak
½ bunch (approx. 4½ oz./125 g)
dinosaur kale
3 tbsp sesame seeds
2 tbsp cold-pressed canola oil
salt
black pepper, freshly ground

**MARINADE:**
2 garlic cloves
4 tbsp honey
1 lime, finely grated peel and juice
4 tbsp Japanese soy sauce
4 tbsp oyster sauce

**DIRECTIONS:**

1. Slice the steak into thick strips.
2. Peel and finely chop the garlic cloves for the marinade. In a bowl, mix honey, garlic, lime peel and juice, soy, and oyster sauces. Add in the meat, and let it marinate for about 10 minutes.
3. Cut the dinosaur kale into coarse strips. In a dry skillet, toast the sesame seeds over medium heat.
4. Heat some canola oil in a skillet. Remove the meat from the marinade (reserving the marinade) and fry it quickly, about 3 to 4 minutes. Add in the marinade, kale, and sesame seeds toward the end, and season with salt and freshly ground black pepper. Serve immediately.

**WHAT TO DRINK**

The honey and soy sauce impart sweetness, which means we need a beverage to match—brown ale, for example—or else the balance of flavors in this dish will be lost.

# 20. Pork Tenderloin Tonnato with Daikon Slaw

*Replacing the original recipe's veal with light and juicy pork tenderloin makes this recipe far more budget-friendly. Tonnato is also good when served with chicken.*

SERVES 4

*1½ lb. (approx. 1½ lb./600 g) pork tenderloin*
*juice of 1 lemon*
*salt*
*black pepper, freshly ground*
*4 inches (10 cm) daikon radish*
*2 stalks celery*
*½ red onion*
*1 bunch dill*
*olive oil*

TONNATO SAUCE:

*1 can (approx. 7 oz./200 g) tuna fish*
*2 eggs, soft boiled for 2 minutes*
*4–6 anchovies*
*½ tbsp grated lemon peel*
*2 tbsp lemon juice, freshly squeezed*
*2 tbsp capers + 1 tbsp pickling liquid*
*¼ cup olive oil*
*black pepper, freshly ground*

DIRECTIONS:

1. Trim the tenderloin. Rub it with lemon juice, and season it all around with salt and pepper.
2. Grill the tenderloin, or sear it in a skillet to give it a nicely browned surface. Finish cooking the meat in a 300°F (150°C) oven until a meat thermometer shows 140°F to 143°F (60°C to 62°C). Let the meat rest for about 5 minutes before slicing it.
3. Peel the daikon radish and julienne it finely. Slice the celery stalks thinly. Peel and thinly slice the red onion. (A kitchen mandolin is very useful for these tasks.) Chop the dill. Place all the vegetables in a bowl and season with salt and olive oil.
4. In a food processor, mix the drained tuna, eggs, anchovies, lemon peel and juice, capers, and pickling liquid. Add the olive oil in a thin stream while continuing to mix, until the sauce becomes thick and smooth. Season with black pepper and perhaps some extra lemon juice.
5. Pour the sauce onto a large platter and place slices of tenderloin on top of sauce. Top with the daikon slaw and a few whole capers; drizzle with olive oil.

**WHAT TO DRINK**
Try a character-rich white wine made from the Pinot Gris grape, or, if you prefer red wine, a Côtes du Rhône with herbal notes and lively acidity.

# 21. Grilled Rib-Eye Steak with Honey-Infused Onions and Vinegar Butter

*Choose a few very good and well-marbled steaks; the fat enhances the flavor immeasurably. This is a far cry from Meatless Monday—and it's Friday, after all!*

**SERVES 4**

4 (about 7 oz./200 g each) rib-eye steaks
sea salt
black pepper, freshly ground

**HONEY-INFUSED ONIONS:**
9 oz. (250 g) pearl onions
9 oz. (250 g) red roasting onions
1–2 tbsp cold-pressed canola oil
2 tbsp honey
juice of 1 lemon
salt
black pepper, freshly ground

**VINEGAR BUTTER:**
5¼ oz. (150 g) unsalted butter
1 shallot
2 tsp apple cider vinegar
salt
black pepper, freshly ground

**DIRECTIONS:**

1. Rub the meat with salt and pepper

**HONEY-SCENTED ONIONS:**

2. Peel the pearl onions and the roasting onions, and sauté them whole in a Dutch oven with some canola oil. Add in the honey and lemon juice, and add water until it covers the onions midway up. Cover with a lid, and let the onions simmer until tender, about 10 minutes. Remove the lid and cook the onions until the liquid has reduced to a thick syrup. Season with salt and pepper.

**VINEGAR BUTTER:**

3. Cream the butter until soft. Peel and finely chop the shallot. Mix the butter and shallot, and season with vinegar, salt, and pepper.

**TO SERVE:**

4. Grill the steaks on a hot grill or hot grill pan, about 3 to 5 minutes on each side. Let the meat rest for a few minutes.

5. Serve meat with the honey-scented onions and a pat of vinegar butter.

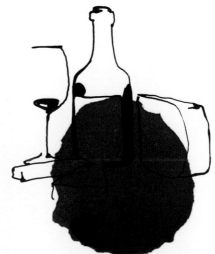

**WHAT TO DRINK**

Vinegar butter softens wine's dryness and enhances its acidity, so to complement the flavor of grilled food, select an acidic wine with oak-barrel notes, such as a classic Rioja or an American Zinfandel.

## 22. Lemon-Roasted Chicken Hindquarters with Spinach and Beet Salad

*This is a fresh, clean dish that will give you a good night's sleep. If you've never used mirin before, here's your chance to try it. Before long, this sweet Japanese rice wine will have a prominent place in your kitchen.*

**SERVES 4**

*4 chicken hindquarters, skin on*
SPINACH AND BEET SALAD:
*2 large beets, cooked*
*1 bag (approx. 2½ oz./70 g)*
*ready-to-use spinach leaves*
*2 salad onions*
*2–3 tbsp fresh horseradish, grated*
*1 tbsp olive oil*
*salt*
*black pepper, freshly ground*

MARINADE:
*3 tbsp olive oil*
*3 tbsp lemon juice, freshly squeezed*
*3 tbsp mirin*
*salt*
*white pepper, freshly ground*

**DIRECTIONS:**

1. Preheat the oven to 350°F (175°C).
2. Mix all ingredients together for the marinade.
3. Place the chicken pieces in an ovenproof dish and pour the marinade over them. Set the dish in the oven and let the chicken bake for 40 minutes. About 3 to 5 minutes before time is up, turn on the oven's broiler to let the skin crisp.
4. Peel and slice the beets thinly with a kitchen mandolin. Put the slices in a bowl along with the spinach. Slice the salad onions thinly and add to the beets. Season with grated horseradish, olive oil, salt, and freshly ground black pepper.
5. Serve chicken warm with the salad.

**WHAT TO DRINK**

In this light chicken dish, the beets' sweetness is very prominent, so choose a beverage with a touch of sweetness and acidity. Why not give a semidry cider from Brittany (Bretagne) a go, or a pale lager, or a slightly full-bodied white wine? Keep in mind that horseradish and wine aren't the best of friends, so reduce the amount of horseradish in the dish if you'll be drinking wine with your meal.

# Whipping It Up on the Sofa

*It's time to dust off the hot toddy and give it back its rightful place in the sitting room again. As a kid, I preferred to eat whipped cream straight from the spoon rather than in a toddy; plus, it was always someone else who whipped the cream. Now, as an adult, I consider making a toddy a moment of pure food Zen. Here I offer you two toddies for adults and one for kids, so set down a towel on the white sofa, and let the whole family join in the whisking!*

## 23. Orange Toddy

SERVES 4

*¼ cup (½ dl) brown sugar*
*1¼ cup (3 dl) water*
*½ orange, grated peel and juice*
*4 oz. (12 cl) smoky whiskey or rum*
*2 eggs*

DIRECTIONS:

1. In a saucepan, bring the sugar, water, orange juice, and peel to a boil. Remove from the heat, and add in smoky whiskey or rum.
2. Whip the eggs to soft peaks with the rest of the sugar, and add them to the sugar/alcohol syrup. Serve in glasses.

## 24. Toddy with Marshmallow Fluff and Nutmeg

SERVES 4

*4 oz. (12 cl) brandy*
*½ cup (1 dl) sweetened condensed milk*
*2 eggs*
*¾ cup (2 dl) warm water*
*2 tbsp marshmallow fluff*
*grated nutmeg, for garnish*

DIRECTIONS:

1. Blend or shake together brandy, condensed milk, and eggs. Add the warm water, and blend or shake again.
2. Pour into glasses. Add a dollop of marshmallow fluff and grate nutmeg on top.

## 25. Chocolate and Coconut Toddy

SERVES 4

*3½ oz. (100 g) milk chocolate*
*1¾ cups (4 dl/1 can) coconut milk*
*1 bunch mint*
*2 eggs*
*1 Hershey's chocolate bar, crushed*

DIRECTIONS:

1. Chop the milk chocolate into small pieces.
2. Bring the coconut milk and some sprigs of mint to a boil, and pour over the chopped chocolate. Stir until the chocolate has melted.
3. Whip the eggs until they are light and airy with soft peaks, and fold them into the chocolate mixture. Pour into glasses and sprinkle with crushed Hershey's bar and sprigs of mint.

26.

27.

## 26. Syllabub with Lemon Curd

Syllabub was a popular dessert in England during the eighteenth and nineteenth centuries. It is reminiscent of an Italian "zabaglione." Of course, you can use store-bought curd, but for those who prefer to make this dessert from scratch, you'll get the recipe right here. You can spread leftovers on your breakfast toast; the lemon curd will keep for about a week in the refrigerator.

SERVES 4

SYLLABUB:

*1¼ cup (3 dl) whipping cream*
*¾ cup (1½ dl) sweet white dessert wine*
*4 Savoiardi cookies (ladyfingers)*

LEMON CURD:

*¼ cup (½ dl) lemon juice*
*1 lemon peel, finely grated*
*¼ cup (½ dl) superfine granulated sugar*
*2 egg yolks*
*1 oz. (25 g) unsalted butter, room temperature*

DIRECTIONS:

1. In a saucepan, whisk together the lemon juice and peel, sugar, and egg yolks for the lemon curd. Bring to a boil while whisking continuously. Let it simmer for a few minutes while the mixture thickens. Remove the saucepan from the heat and add in butter bit by bit. Stir until the curd is nice and smooth. Let it cool in the refrigerator.
2. Whip the cream until it forms soft peaks. Fold in 3 tablespoons lemon curd and wine.
3. Pour into glasses and serve with the ladyfinger cookies. Drink the same sweet wine with this syllabub as you used to prepare the dessert.

## 27. Frozen Fruit Salad

This is the very best everyday dessert—my kids love it! I can guarantee that this fruit salad will turn all sour pusses into happy faces.

SERVES 4

*1 small pineapple*
*¼ small watermelon*
*2 pears*
*2 passion fruits*

DIRECTIONS:

1. Peel the pineapple, watermelon, and pears, and stash them in the freezer for 2 to 3 hours.
2. Remove the fruit from the freezer and grate them coarsely with a box grater. Transfer to plates and spoon the passion fruit over them. Dig in immediately!

## 28. Banana-Yogurt Ice Cream with Coffee-Toffee Sauce

Layer the delicious banana ice cream with the sweet toffee sauce and crushed biscotti, and you have trifle in a glass.

MAKES ABOUT 2 CUPS(½ LITER/5 DL)
BANANA-YOGURT ICE CREAM:

*4 bananas*
*¾ cup (2 dl) Russian yogurt, such as Pavel's (17% fat content)*
*¼ cup (½ dl) confectioner's sugar*
*1 lemon, grated peel and juice*
*biscotti, crushed, for serving*

COFFEE-TOFFEE SAUCE:

*3½ oz. (100 g) brown sugar*
*3½ oz. (100 g) unsalted butter*
*¾ cup (2 dl) whipping cream*
*1¼ cup (2½ dl) dark syrup or molasses*
*2 tbsp coffee beans, coarsely crushed*
*½ lemon, grated peel and juice*

DIRECTIONS:

1. Peel and slice the bananas, and store them in the freezer for several hours.
2. In a saucepan, mix all ingredients for the sauce and let the mixture simmer for 15 to 20 minutes, until it becomes a thick toffee sauce. Strain out the coffee beans if you prefer a completely smooth sauce.
3. In a food processor, blend the chilled bananas with the yogurt, confectioner's sugar, lemon peel, and lemon juice, until it becomes a smooth and light ice cream.
4. Serve immediately with coffee-toffee sauce and crushed biscotti.

## 29. Raspberry-Mascarpone Ice Cream with Raspberry Licorice Sauce

I've begun to appreciate the combination of raspberry and licorice more and more with age. These days, this relative newcomer among flavor combos has a safe place both in the grocery store and in our hearts.

MAKES ABOUT 2 CUPS (½ LITER/5 DL)
RASPBERRY MASCARPONE ICE CREAM:

*8 oz. (225 g) frozen raspberries*
*9 oz. (250 g) mascarpone*
*½ lemon, grated peel and juice*
*½ cup (1 dl) confectioner's sugar*
*2 tsp vanilla sugar*
*biscotti, crushed, for serving*

RASPBERRY-LICORICE SAUCE:

*8 oz. (225 g) frozen raspberries*
*⅓ cup (2½ oz./¾ dl) confectioner's sugar*
*4 tbsp licorice powder*
*1 tbsp lemon juice*

DIRECTIONS:

1. To make the sauce, use an immersion blender to mix the raspberries, confectioner's sugar, licorice powder, and lemon juice. Strain the raspberry seeds to make a thick, smooth sauce.
2. In a food processor, quickly mix all the ice cream ingredients together to make a light and smooth ice cream.
3. Serve ice cream immediately with the raspberry-licorice sauce and crushed biscotti.

29.

28.

Saturday

*It's Saturday, finally!*
I love Saturday dinners—it's so much fun to prepare good food, lay a pretty table, and dress up. At our house, we always put on our best clothes for the occasion: a good dress, high heels, and for the men, a suit— even if only our family is in attendance. Saturdays need not to be complicated to be enjoyable, however. Throw a roast in the oven for a few hours, or let a pot simmer away slowly on the stove while you're busy with other things, and the dinner will almost take care of itself.

31.

33.

# While Your Guests Are Mingling . . .

*Passing around some tasty snacks before you sit down to dinner will garner you some serious brownie points from your guests and will put everyone in a festive mood. This also buys you some extra time for last-minute touches in the kitchen. All too often, we hurry the meal because children get hungry, so let them dig in while the grown-ups enjoy some hot edamame or corn on the cob rolled in butter or cheese.*

## 30. Edamame Fried in Sumac and Chili

Only buy edamame that is certified organic so you avoid ingesting a lot of weird additives.

SERVES 4

 1 bag (approx. 1 lb./450 g) frozen edamame
 2 tsp crushed sumac
 3 tbsp olive oil
 ½ tsp chili flakes
 sea salt

DIRECTIONS:

1. Heat olive oil and chili flakes in a skillet, and add in edamame and sumac. Sauté for a few minutes until the edamame has warmed through. Season with sea salt.
2. Place the edamame in a bowl or on a platter and serve warm. A Japanese pale lager makes a perfect accompaniment.

## 31. Beet Tartlets with Sheep's Milk Cheese and Maple Syrup

This goes nicely with a slightly sweet beer, if the tartlets are to be eaten as a main course.

SERVES 4

 2 sheets frozen puff pastry
 5¼ oz. (150 g) sheep's or goat's milk cheese
 1–2 beets, cooked
 ½ lemon, grated peel
 2–3 tbsp maple syrup
 salt
 black pepper, freshly ground
 1 beaten egg, for glazing
 2 tbsp pine nuts

DIRECTIONS:

1. Preheat the oven to 480°F (250°C).
2. Cut the pastry sheets into four squares. At a generous ⅓ inch (approx. 1 cm) in from the edge, cut a fine line, not quite through, along all sides. Transfer the pastry to a baking sheet lined with parchment paper.
3. Slice the beets. Place the cheese in the middle of the pastry squares, and sprinkle with grated lemon peel. Cover with slices of beets. Drizzle with maple syrup and season with salt and pepper. Brush the edges of the pastry with the beaten egg.
4. Bake in the oven about 10 to 12 minutes, until the pastry is golden brown and crisp, and the maple syrup has caramelized.
5. Meanwhile, roast the pine nuts in a dry skillet. Keep an eye on them so they don't burn!
6. Place the tartlets on a cutting board or platter, and sprinkle with toasted pine nuts. Serve immediately.

## 32. Warm Tomatoes and Grapes with Parmesan Breadsticks

If you like croutons, you'll cheer for this Parmesan bread!

SERVES 4

 *10½ oz. (300 g) green grapes*
 *10½ oz. (300 g) mix of small, ripe tomatoes*
 *3 tbsp olive oil*
 *2 garlic cloves, crushed*
 *3 tbsp honey*
 *2 tsp salt*
 *black pepper, freshly ground*
 *1 bunch Italian parsley, chopped*

PARMESAN BREAD

 *sourdough bread*
 *2½ oz. (75 g) butter*
 *2 tsp Dijon mustard*
 *1¾ oz. (50 g) Parmesan, grated*

DIRECTIONS:

1. Preheat the oven to 390°F (200°C).
2. Place all ingredients up to the parsley in an ovenproof dish and stir with a spoon. Place the dish in the oven for about 10 to 15 minutes. The tomatoes and grapes should soften a little.
3. Remove the dish from the oven and add in chopped parsley.
4. Increase the oven temperature to 445°F (230°C).
5. Cut the bread into thick oblong strips, and place them in a bowl. Melt the butter and mix in the mustard. Pour the butter-mustard mixture over the bread and turn the pieces while coating with Parmesan. Set the pieces of bread on a rack with a baking sheet underneath, and roast the breadsticks about 20 minutes or until the pieces are golden brown.
6. Place the tomatoes and grapes in individual bowls and serve them with the Parmesan bread. Dip bread into the juices from the tomatoes and grapes.

**WHAT TO DRINK**
Try a fruity Prosecco, with a slight crisp sweetness and flowery note.

## 33. Deep-Fried Avocado with Lemon Dip and Peanuts

This is a dish I served to Israeli chef Eyal Shanni when I visited Tel Aviv. He enjoyed it, and I'm sure you will, too!

SERVES 4

*3–4 avocados*

*1¾ cups (4 dl) panko breadcrumbs, for breading*

*oil, for frying*

*½ cup (1 dl) roasted peanuts, chopped*

BATTER:

*¾ cup (2 dl) carbonated water*

*¾ cup (2 dl) all-purpose flour*

*½ tsp salt*

*1 tbsp honey*

*2 tbsp baking powder*

LEMON DIP:

*2 egg yolks*

*2 tsp sweet, strong mustard*

*1 lemon, grated peel + 1 tbsp lemon juice*

*1¼ cup (3 dl) unflavored canola oil*

*¼ tsp salt*

*Tabasco, to taste*

*1–2 tbsp crème fraîche*

DIRECTIONS:

1. In a bowl, mix all ingredients for the batter, and set aside.
2. Stir together the egg yolks, mustard, grated lemon peel and juice for the dip. Add the oil drop by drop while whisking constantly, until the sauce thickens. Season with salt and Tabasco, and finish by whisking in some crème fraîche to add body to the sauce.
3. Peel the avocados and remove the pits. Cut each avocado into 4 wedges.
4. In a large saucepan, heat the oil to 320°F (160°C).
5. Coat the avocado wedges in the batter, and then into the panko crumbs. Deep-fry the wedges until golden brown and crispy, and then let them drain on paper towels.
6. Place the deep-fried wedges on a platter and serve them with the dip. Top with chopped peanuts.

**WHAT TO DRINK**

Drink a pale lager with this avocado dish, preferably one with citrusy and fruity notes.

*Go on—don't chicken out!
This avocado dish is not at all
difficult to make!*

## 34. Corn On the Cob with Browned Parsley Butter

An American pale lager is just the thing to savor with corn on the cob.

SERVES 4

*4 ears of corn on the cob*
*salt, for the cooking water*

BROWNED PARSLEY BUTTER:

*2 shallots*
*2–3 garlic cloves*
*7 oz. (200 g) butter*
*2 large eggs, soft-boiled for 2 minutes*
*1 tbsp Dijon mustard*
*2 tbsp lemon juice*
*½–¾ cup (1½–2 dl) olive oil*
*salt*
*black pepper, freshly ground*
*1 bunch Italian parsley, chopped*

DIRECTIONS:

1. Peel and slice the shallots. Peel the garlic cloves. Fry shallots and garlic in some of the butter until they are nicely browned.
2. Brown the butter until it is golden and there are no more bubbles. Let it cool. Transfer the shallots and butter into a bowl (such as a stainless steel measuring vessel) and blend with an immersion blender until the mixture is smooth.
3. Cut the soft-boiled eggs in half, and scoop out the yolks with a spoon. Mix egg yolks, mustard, and lemon juice in a container, and blend with an immersion blender. Add the browned onion butter and olive oil in a thin stream until the sauce has thickened like a mayonnaise, adding a few drips of lukewarm water if the sauce is too thick. Season with salt, pepper, and additional lemon juice to taste.
4. Cook the ears of corn in salted water (the water should taste very salty, so don't hold back on the salt) for about 5 to 7 minutes.
5. Place the cooked corn on a platter, roll them in the butter sauce and chopped parsley, and serve immediately.

## 35. Corn On the Cob with Parmesan Cheese and Black Pepper

There are no words for this other than: absolutely yummy!

SERVES 4

*4 ears of corn*
*salt, for the cooking water*
*5¼ oz. (150 g) Parmesan cheese*
*2 tbsp butter*
*black pepper, freshly ground*

DIRECTIONS:

1. Cook the corn in salted water (the water should taste very salty, so don't hold back on the salt) for about 5 to 7 minutes. Meanwhile, grate the cheese.
2. Place the corn on a platter and roll them in butter. Sprinkle with grated cheese and season with freshly ground black pepper. Serve immediately.

# 36. Crisp-Fried Baltic Herring with Cucumber & Celery Salsa

*Try serving the dish on a slice of buttered dark rye bread for an al fresco lunch, or as part of a buffet table. The choice is up to you—as it should be!*

**SERVES 4**

*12 small Baltic herrings or brislings*
*12 small sprat fillets*
*2 eggs*
*¾ cup (2 dl) panko breadcrumbs*
*black pepper, freshly ground*
*¼–½ cup (½–1 dl) oil, for frying*

**CUCUMBER & CELERY SALSA**
*½ English (or hothouse) cucumber*
*3 stalks celery*
*1 scallion*
*1 small spring onion*
*1 small green chili*
*1 tsp cumin*
*4 tbsp parsley or cilantro, coarsely chopped*
*green Tabasco, to taste*
*2 limes, grated peel and juice*
*salt*
*fruity olive oil, for serving*

**DIRECTIONS:**

1. For the salsa, peel and remove the seeds from the cucumber. Finely dice cucumber, celery, scallion, onion, and chili. In a bowl, mix the diced vegetables with cumin and parsley or cilantro. Season with Tabasco, lime, and salt.

2. Cut open and lay flat each herring, and place a sprat fillet on each. Season with black pepper and fold the fish up together again.

3. Lightly whisk the eggs with a fork. Dip the fish, first in egg wash, and then in the breadcrumbs.

4. Fry the herrings until crisp, about 2 to 3 minutes on each side, until they are heated through. Let them drain on paper towels.

5. Transfer the salsa to glasses, and top with the herring. Drizzle with some fruity olive oil and serve immediately while the fish is freshly crisp and warm.

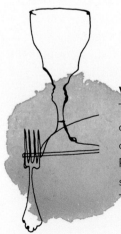

**WHAT TO DRINK**

The dominant flavors here are lime, chili, herbs, and sweetness, so it makes sense to pair this dish with a New Zealand Sauvignon Blanc. Remember the wine should be a bit on the sweet side to balance out the heat from the chili and Tabasco.

# 37. Salt-Roasted Beets with Petite Lobster (Scampi), with Dill & Garlic Crème

*A great way to prepare beets and most other root vegetables is to salt-roast them. They become juicy, taste heavenly, and can be eaten either hot or cold. Why not try throwing in a carrot or a chunk of celeriac (celery root) into the salt, too? After all, celeriac makes a wonderful side dish for Petite lobsters.*

**SERVES 4**

*8 small beets, green leaves left intact*
*4 large, uncooked Petite lobsters*
*kosher salt*
*2 tbsp olive oil and butter, for frying*
*black pepper, freshly ground*

**DILL & GARLIC CRÈME**
*3 garlic cloves*
*large bunch of dill*
*1¼ cups (3 dl) cold-pressed canola oil*
*2 egg yolks*
*2 tsp Dijon mustard*
*1 tsp white wine vinegar*
*salt*
*white pepper, freshly ground*

**GARNISH:**
*reserved dill crowns*

**DIRECTIONS:**

1. Preheat the oven to 350°F (175°C).
2. Scrub the beets clean, but leave their green tops on. Spread some coarse salt in a baking pan. Coat the beets in olive oil, place them in the salt, and cover them lightly with some more salt.
3. Bake the beets for about 30 to 40 minutes, until soft. Test with a toothpick to check for doneness.
4. Cut the beets in halves or quarters, and season them with freshly ground black pepper. Set aside.
5. Peel the Petite lobster tails. Save and freeze the heads and claws for later use in soup or stock.
6. Peel the garlic cloves and chop the dill, including some of the stalks. Heat the oil to 150°F (65°C)—it has to be hot! With an immersion blender, mix the warm oil with the garlic and dill until you have smooth, green oil. Let the oil cool.
7. Whisk the egg yolks with mustard and vinegar and some salt, and add the green oil drop by drop until the sauce has thickened. Season with salt and white pepper. Chill the crème in the refrigerator.
8. Transfer the beets to glasses. In a hot skillet, quickly fry the Petite lobster tails, back-side down, for about 30 seconds, in olive oil and butter. Turn and quickly cook the other side, and then place the tails on top of the beets. Spoon dill and garlic crème over the lobsters and beets, and garnish with the reserved dill crowns.

**WHAT TO DRINK**
A sparkling wine with delicate sweetness and fresh fruit notes complements Petite lobster's natural sweet and salty flavor.

## 38. Veal Filet Mignon Tartare with Capers, Horseradish, and Quail's Eggs

*Make sure to use a high-quality veal filet mignon for this tartare. Ask your butcher to recommend good cuts for best results.*

SERVES 4

10½ oz. (300 g) veal filet mignon, trimmed
1 shallot
1 garlic clove
2 tsp capers
2 tsp coarse-grain Dijon mustard
8 quail eggs
¼ lemon, grated peel and juice
2 tbsp olive oil
salt, to taste
black pepper, freshly ground
1 bunch nasturtium leaves, for garnish
fresh horseradish, grated

DIRECTIONS:

1. Finely chop the meat.
2. Peel and finely chop the shallot and garlic clove. Transfer the shallot, garlic clove, capers, and mustard to a mortar and mash with a pestle.
3. Boil the quail eggs for 2 minutes. Cool them immediately in cold water, and then peel them carefully. Cut them in half when ready to serve.
4. Mix the meat with the caper mixture, and season with grated lemon peel and juice, olive oil, salt, and pepper.
5. Place the tartare in Champagne glasses. Top each glass with half a quail's egg, coarsely grated horseradish, and nasturtium leaves.

**WHAT TO DRINK**

Beer goes best with steak tartare. Choose a lager with some acidity to it, since capers and lemon are both acidic. Or opt for a fresh and tart apple cider instead, if you prefer to go alcohol free.

# 39. Lamb Stew with Walnuts, Dates, and Herbed Couscous

*I love fruit and nuts in my dishes! Well, I don't go for banana on my pizza; you have to draw the line somewhere . . .*

### SERVES 4

1¾ lb. (800 g) boneless leg of lamb
1 head of garlic
1 small celeriac (celery root)
1 eggplant
2 yellow onions
olive oil and butter, for frying
¼ cup (½ dl) tikka masala
(optional: garam masala spice
paste)
salt
black pepper, freshly ground
2 cans (14 oz./400 g each)
crushed tomatoes
¾ cup (2 dl) water
¾ cup (2 dl) walnuts, crushed
12 fresh dates, cut into strips

### HERBED COUSCOUS

1 shallot, sliced
1 bunch Italian parsley
1 bunch cilantro
1 bunch (1 oz./30 g) arugula
½ lb. (250 g) couscous
juice from ½ lemon
salt
black pepper, freshly ground

### DIRECTIONS:

1. Cut the lamb into stew-sized chunks, roughly 1 inch around. Peel and crush the garlic cloves. Peel and cut the celeriac into wedges. Cut the eggplant into even-sized wedges. Peel and coarsely chop the yellow onions.

2. In a skillet, brown the meat in batches with olive oil and butter along with the garlic, onion, and spices. Transfer the cooked meat to a Dutch oven as you go. Pour the crushed tomatoes and water into the pot and bring to a boil.

3. Add in the celeriac and eggplant. Cover, and let simmer for about 50 minutes, or until the meat is tender.

### HERBED COUSCOUS

4. In a food processor, finely chop the onion, parsley, cilantro, and arugula. Add in the couscous and pulse twice—the couscous should remain intact.

5. In a saucepan, bring 2 cups (½ liter/5 dl) of water with ½ teaspoon salt to a boil. Pour the water over the couscous in the food processor, and let sit for a few minutes.

6. Fluff the couscous with a fork and season with squeezed lemon juice, salt, and pepper.

### TO SERVE:

7. Stir the roasted walnuts and the date strips into the stew, and serve with a side of herbed couscous.

**WHAT TO DRINK**
Choose a full-bodied red wine with herby notes, such as an Australian Shiraz.

40.

# 40. Overnight Chuck Roast with Morel Sauce, Lemon-Roasted Root Vegetables, and Rowanberry Jelly

*I love food that cooks while I sleep. I also like the "see you later, alligator" post-work meal. This meal takes care of itself while you work or are otherwise occupied.*

### SERVES 4

3¼ lb. (1500 g) chuck roast
¾ cup (2 dl) BBQ sauce
2 tbsp white wine vinegar
1 tbsp paprika
⅖ tsp cayenne pepper

### MOREL SAUCE:

3½ oz. dried morel mushrooms
1 shallot
½ tbsp butter
¾ cup (1½ dl) white wine
½ cup (1 dl) water
1¼ cups (2½ dl) heavy cream
3 tbsp salt
white pepper, freshly ground

### DIRECTIONS:

1. Preheat the oven to 250°F (120°C).
2. Mix together BBQ sauce, vinegar, paprika, and cayenne pepper. Set the roast in a thick-bottomed Dutch oven and pour the sauce over it. Turn the meat until it is completely coated by the sauce. Place a lid on the pot, place it in the oven, and leave it to cook for about 6 to 8 hours. The meat is ready when it falls apart. So, off to bed or work you go!

### MOREL SAUCE:

3. Peel and slice the shallot. Parboil the morels twice in boiling water, changing the water each time. Pour off the water and let the morels drain on paper towels. Chop them coarsely and sauté them in butter with the onion. Add the wine and water, and let it cook and reduce to half the volume. Add in the heavy cream and cook until the sauce is creamy. Season with salt and pepper.

**LEMON-ROASTED ROOT VEGETABLES:**

1 bag (10½ oz./330 g) yellow pearl onions
2 parsnips
1 bunch carrots
6–8 tender parsley roots
1 lemon
¼ cup (½ dl) honey
olive oil
1 bunch parsley
salt
black pepper, freshly ground

## LEMON-ROASTED ROOT VEGETABLES:

4. Preheat the oven to 355°F (180°C).

5. Peel the onions and scrub the root vegetables clean. Cut the parsnips into large chunks, leaving the rest of the vegetables intact (if they're especially large, however, cut them in half through the middle).

6. Put the vegetables on a rimmed baking sheet. Cut the lemon in half and squeeze it over the vegetables, then drizzle with honey and olive oil. Cut the lemon halves into smaller pieces and add them to the vegetables. Toss all the vegetables with your hands. Season with salt and pepper.

7. Roast the vegetable for 25 to 30 minutes. Stir the contents or shake the baking sheet a few times while roasting so everything cooks and roasts evenly. Don't overcook them—slightly al dente is good. Chop the parsley and add it to the vegetables.

### TO SERVE:

8. Spoon the morel sauce onto a large platter and set the meat on top. Serve with the lemon-roasted root vegetables and a dollop of rowanberry jelly.

**WHAT TO DRINK**

Here is a hearty dish that can stand up to rustic, deep-flavored wines, thanks to the morel sauce. A concentrated, full-bodied Bordeaux from Pomerol is a good choice.

41

# 41. Roast Sirloin with Hasselback Potatoes, Red Wine Sauce, and Grandma's Green Tomatoes

*Plan to make the pickled tomatoes one week in advance, as they need to marinate for a while to really come into their own.*

**SERVES 4**

1¾ lb. (800 g) whole sirloin roast
butter and olive oil, for frying
sea salt
black pepper, freshly ground

HASSELBACK POTATOES:
1¾ lb. (800 g) small potatoes
(fingerling or heirloom)
4 tbsp olive oil
2 tbsp breadcrumbs
salt
black pepper, freshly ground

RED WINE SAUCE:
1 red onion
3 garlic cloves
1 carrot
1 parsnip
1 slice smoked pork belly
2½ cups (6 dl) red wine
2 cups (5 dl) beef stock
3 tbsp Japanese soy sauce
2 tbsp olive oil
3–4 tbsp unsalted butter
salt
black pepper, freshly ground
1 tbsp cornstarch, for thickening the
sauce (optional)

**DIRECTIONS:**

1. Preheat the oven to 265°F (130°C).
2. In a pan, brown the roast in butter and oil. Season with salt and pepper. Place the meat on a rack with a rimmed baking sheet underneath to catch the drippings. Place a meat thermometer in the roast, and bake until the thermometer reads 129.2°F to 132.4°F (54°C to 56°C) and the meat is a delicate pink.
3. Remove the meat from the oven and let it rest while you prepare the potatoes and the sauce.

HASSELBACK POTATOES:

4. Preheat the oven to 390°F (200°C).
5. Use a small sharp knife and make several small thin cuts (but do not cut all the way through) in the potatoes. Place the potatoes in a bowl with olive oil, breadcrumbs, salt, and pepper and stir until they are thoroughly coated. Place the potatoes, slit-side up, in a baking pan and bake for 35 to 40 minutes, or until the potatoes are golden and crisp.

RED WINE SAUCE:

6. Peel onion and garlic and dice them together with the root vegetables and smoked pork belly. Brown all of it in butter and olive oil in a thick-bottomed pan. Add the wine, and let simmer for about 10 minutes. Add the beef stock and soy sauce, and let it cook and reduce to half the original volume, about 25 to 30 minutes.
7. Strain the sauce, and season with salt and black pepper; add in the rest of the butter, piece by piece. If you prefer a thicker sauce, add in some cornstarch diluted in water.

**GRANDMA'S GREEN TOMATOES:**

*2 ¼ lbs. (1000 g) green tomatoes*
*4 cups (1 liter/10 dl) water*
*1½ tbsp salt*
*1¼ inch (3 cm) fresh ginger*
*3 garlic cloves*
*2 cups white vinegar*
*1¾ cups (4 dl) superfine*
*granulated sugar*
*2 cinnamon sticks*
*10 allspice peppercorns*
*1 tbsp yellow mustard seed*

**DIRECTIONS:**

8. Bring the water and salt to a boil. Cut the tomatoes in half and let them cook in the water for 30 seconds to 1 minute. Rinse them quickly under running cold water and then remove their skins.

9. Slice the ginger and garlic. In a saucepan, mix the slices with the rest of the ingredients for the preserving liquid, and bring it all to a boil. Add the tomatoes and let them simmer for 5 minutes. Remove the tomatoes and transfer them to thoroughly cleaned glass jars. Strain the liquid and pour it over the tomatoes. Let them steep for 24 hours.

10. Pour off the preserving liquid into a saucepan and bring it to a boil, carefully skimming the foam from the surface. Again, pour the hot liquid over the tomatoes and close the jars. Let them steep at least 24 hours before using. The longer they sit in the juice, the tastier and more full-bodied they will become. The tomatoes will keep for about a month in the refrigerator.

**TO SERVE:**

11. Warm the roast in a still-warm oven about 5 to 8 minutes. Remove the roast and slice it into nice slices. Serve with pickled tomatoes, Hasselback potatoes, and red wine sauce. By all means, add a small green salad to the meal, too.

### WHAT TO DRINK

A young, fruity red wine is generally recommended for red wine sauces, as oak barrel-aged wine can often leave an undesirable, bitter aftertaste when used in sauces. With this dish, you are free to choose just about any red wine you like, but my tip here is to go for a fruity Chilean Cabernet Sauvignon—delicious!

## 42. Tina's Crispy Pork Roast with Red Cabbage and Coarse-Grain Mustard

*Word is that this pork roast is as Danish as Queen Margarethe herself. But my pig speaks Swedish, not Danish, and that's that!*

**SERVES 4**

*3¼ lb. (1500 g) boneless pork roast*
*1–2 tbsp Kosher salt*
*1 bag prunes*
*4– 6 garlic cloves, slivered*
*black pepper, freshly ground*

**RED CABBAGE:**
*1 small head red cabbage*
*½ tbsp salt*
*2 generous slices of smoked pork belly or bacon*
*¾ cup (2 dl) water*
*2½ oz. (¾ dl) apple cider vinegar*
*½ cup (1 dl) dry white wine*
*1 yellow onion, sliced*
*1 apple, grated*
*2 tsp caraway seeds*
*3 bay leaves*
*salt*
*black pepper, freshly ground*

**DIRECTIONS:**

1. Preheat the oven to 350°F (175°C).
2. Cut a few slits through the pork's rind lengthwise to make a pattern. Rub the rind with salt, and make sure that it enters into all the slits thoroughly. Then cut small pockets into the meat and insert the prunes and garlic slivers. Finish by seasoning the roast all over with black pepper.
3. Cover the bottom of a small roasting pan with water and place the roast rind-side down in the water. Insert a meat thermometer into the roast and bake it on the middle rack of the oven for 15 minutes.
4. Remove the roast from the oven and place it, rind-side up, on a rack in a baking pan. Continue baking the roast until the thermometer reads 340°F (172°C). You can increase the oven's temperature to 480°F (250°C), and also use the broiling setting for the last 5 minutes to make the rind extra crispy, but be careful it doesn't burn!

**RED CABBAGE:**

5. Julienne the cabbage with a kitchen mandolin and place the strips in a large colander. Salt the cabbage, turning it over a few times and then letting it sit for 10 to 15 minutes. Wring out the liquid from the cabbage. Dice the pork belly or bacon.
6. In a saucepan, bring the water, vinegar, and wine together with the onion, apple, and spices to a boil. Add in the cabbage and place a lid on the pan. Bring back to a boil, and then lower the heat and let simmer for 30 to 35 minutes. Season with more salt and pepper if needed. Take care not to overcook—the cabbage should be slightly al dente.

**TO SERVE:**

7. Slice the meat and place it attractively on a platter together with the red cabbage. Serve with boiled potatoes, coarse-grained mustard, bread, and a nice beer. A good choice would be a Swedish or Danish craft beer with acidity, fruit, and slightly bitter finish. Or, a spicy American Pinot Noir wine.

## 43. Curried Chicken with Sweet Potatoes, Roasted Chickpeas, and Mint

*I love to cook one-pot dishes where all ingredients come together for that full-flavored taste. Roasted chickpeas add a satisfying crunch, while the mint makes it fresh.*

**SERVES 4**

1 large chicken
2 sweet potatoes
1 yellow onion
1 whole head garlic
3 tbsp curry powder
1 tsp whole black peppercorns
1 tbsp yellow mustard seeds
½ tsp green cardamom
butter and oil, for frying
rind of 1 lemon, thinly peeled
½ lemon, juice
4 cups (1 liter/10 dl) water or chicken stock
cornstarch and water mixture
sea salt

GARNISH AND TO SERVE:
½ cup (1 dl) crushed roasted chickpeas
1 bunch fresh mint
¾ cup (2 dl) natural yogurt (10% fat)
naan bread

**DIRECTIONS:**

1. Cut the chicken into approximately 8 pieces. Peel the sweet potatoes and cut them in large chunks. Peel and cut the onion into wedges and cut the garlic head in half, straight across.

2. Cook the curry powder, black pepper, mustard seed, and cardamom for a few minutes in a large pot with a little butter and oil. Add in the chicken pieces and brown them lightly in the curry butter.

3. Add in the onion and the rest of the ingredients; add water or stock so it barely covers the pot's contents. Put a lid on the pot and bring to a boil, and simmer gently for 30 to 35 minutes, or until the meat falls off the bones and the potatoes are soft. Thicken the sauce with a little cornstarch. Season with salt.

4. Sprinkle the curry with chickpeas and mint leaves. Serve, preferably with some plain yogurt and warm naan bread.

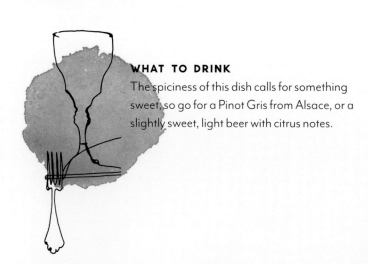

**WHAT TO DRINK**
The spiciness of this dish calls for something sweet, so go for a Pinot Gris from Alsace, or a slightly sweet, light beer with citrus notes.

# 44. Whole Baked Salmon with Butter Sauce, Riced Potatoes, and Spinach Salad

*Fish is a quick and easy meal, not labor intensive. On the other hand, butter sauce can be, well, not quite as simple, but we can put in a little effort, right?*

SERVES 4

4½–5½ lbs. (2–2½ kg) whole
Norwegian salmon or rainbow
trout, skin on
sea salt
black pepper, freshly ground
olive oil

RICED POTATOES:
1¾ lbs. peeled potatoes,
preferably starchy
salt for cooking
black pepper, freshly ground

BUTTER SAUCE (BEURRE BLANC):
1 shallot
butter, for frying
¼ cup (½ dl) white wine vinegar
¼ cup (½ dl) dry white wine
1½ oz.(300 g) butter
salt
white pepper, freshly ground
4 tbsp salmon roe
2 tbsp chives, snipped fine

DIRECTIONS:

1. Preheat the oven to 375°F (190°C).
2. Oil a sheet of doubled aluminum foil and fit onto a rimmed baking sheet. Place the salmon on the foil. Make thin incisions all along both sides of the backbone. Rub the fish's belly and sides with some sea salt and freshly ground black pepper. Place a meat thermometer near the bone at the thickest part of the fish.
3. Place the baking sheet in the oven and let the salmon bake for 30 to 35 minutes, or until the thermometer reads 130°F (55°C). Let the fish rest for a few minutes and then loosen the skin carefully. Keep the salmon warm under the foil.

RICED POTATOES:

4. Boil the potatoes in salted water. Pour off the water and keep the potatoes warm in a covered saucepan until serving time.

BUTTER SAUCE:

5. Peel and finely chop the shallot. In a saucepan, cook the shallot in a pat of butter. Add the vinegar and white wine and cook down (reduce) until there are about 3 tablespoons of liquid remaining. Add the butter, piece by piece, while whisking continuously, until the sauce is shiny and smooth. Season with salt and freshly ground white pepper. Add the snipped chives and the roe at serving time.

**SPINACH SALAD:**

*1 bag (approx. 2½ oz./70 g)
baby spinach
1 container pea shoots
1 bunch dill
olive oil
lemon juice, freshly squeezed*

**SPINACH SALAD:**

6. Mix the salad ingredients in a bowl and season with olive oil and some freshly squeezed lemon juice.

**TO SERVE:**

7. Rice the potatoes in batches and season with freshly ground black pepper.

8. Serve the salmon with riced potatoes, butter sauce, and spinach salad.

**WHAT TO DRINK**

Opt for something elegant with salmon, such as a Chardonnay grape, the obvious choice being a Chablis.

# 45. Baked Hake with Jerusalem Artichokes, Bacon, And Horseradish

*This is a dish in which Jerusalem artichokes truly shine. If you've never baked whole Jerusalem artichokes before, now is the time. The sweetness of these roots really blossoms after baking, and their skin turns a beautiful golden brown. Wow, this is making me ravenous!*

**SERVES 4**

1¼–1½ lbs. (600–700 g) Jerusalem artichokes
5 oz. (140 g) bacon
1¾ lbs. (800 g) hake fillets
1 bag (approx. 2½ oz./70 g) arugula
½ cup horseradish, freshly grated
2 tbsp olive oil
½ tbsp sea salt
black pepper, freshly ground

**DIRECTIONS:**

1. Preheat the oven to 435°F (225°C).
2. Scrub the Jerusalem artichokes thoroughly and cut them in half lengthwise if they're large. Place them in an ovenproof dish and drizzle with some olive oil. Lay the bacon slices on top of the artichokes and slide the dish into the oven. Bake for about 30 minutes, or until the artichokes start to get soft.
3. Meanwhile, cut the fish into 8 to 10 medium-sized pieces. Quickly chop together arugula and grated horseradish with a few drops of olive oil to make a dry pesto.
4. Remove the artichokes from the oven; lay the fish over the artichokes and season lightly with salt. Increase the oven temperature to 480°F (250°C) and return the dish to the oven. Bake the fish for another 10 minutes or until white and firm to the touch and the bacon is crisp.
5. Serve the fish directly from the pan, sprinkled with arugula-horseradish pesto.

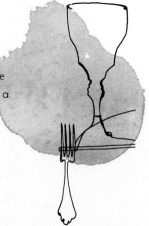

**WHAT TO DRINK**

Dishes containing bacon can handle barrel-aged wines, so why not enjoy a Chenin Blanc from the Loire Valley?

# 46. Saturday Bread with Dip and Butter Glaze

*The dough for this bread is very delicate and needs to be handled with kid gloves. If you want to get a head start, mix the dough the day before and let it rest overnight, well covered, in the refrigerator. Then, carefully separate the dough into pieces and bake immediately! Za'atar is a Middle Eastern spice blend.*

**SATURDAY BREAD:**

¼ packet fresh yeast

5¼ oz. (150 g) sourdough

2¾ cups (6½ dl) cold water

4 cups (1 liter/10 dl) high-gluten wheat flour

¾ cup (2 dl) whole wheat flour

1 tbsp salt

olive oil

**BROWNED WHIPPED BUTTER:**

9 oz. (250 g) unsalted butter

3 tbsp water

¼ cup (½ dl) chopped herbs, such as parsley or French tarragon

sea salt flakes

**ARTICHOKE DIP:**

1 (14 oz./400 g) jar artichoke hearts

2 garlic cloves

1 cup (2½ dl) pitted green olives

1 tbsp capers

2½ oz. (¾ dl) olive oil

salt

black pepper, freshly ground

**ZA'ATAR WITH ALMONDS AND MELTED BUTTER:**

½ cup (1 dl) almonds, blanched and peeled

4 tbsp sesame seeds

2 tbsp sumac

1 tbsp coriander seeds

4 tbsp dried Mediterranean oregano

¾ tsp salt

1¾ oz. (50 g) butter

**DIRECTIONS:**

**SATURDAY BREAD:**

1. Work all the ingredients in a food processor for approximately 10 minutes until you have smooth and elastic dough. Let the dough rest in a large bowl that has been lightly greased with olive oil at room temperature for 1½ to 2 hours.

2. Preheat the oven to 480°F (250°C). Tip the dough carefully out onto a floured work surface or baking board, and, using a dough scraper and scale, cut the dough into equal pieces. Place the pieces of bread on parchment paper and let them rise for another 25 to 30 minutes.

3. Bake the bread (it's a good idea to use a preheated baking sheet) for 12 to 15 minutes. The bread should be puffy and golden brown.

**BROWNED WHIPPED BUTTER:**

4. Brown the butter in a pan, whisking continuously from the bottom and up. When the bubbling subsides and the butter turns golden brown, pour into a metal bowl. Be careful with the bottom residue, as it can continue to cook in the pan.

5. Chill the butter in an ice bath (place the bowl in a larger container or bowl filled with ice water) and, when it begins to cool, add in 3 tablespoons lukewarm water. Beat the butter until light and fluffy. Fold in the herbs and season with sea salt flakes.

**ARTICHOKE DIP:**

6. In a food processor or with an immersion blender, mix all ingredients to make a smooth dip. Season with salt and freshly ground black pepper.

**ZA'ATAR WITH ALMONDS AND MELTED BUTTER:**

7. Roast the almonds and sesame seeds separately in a dry skillet until golden brown. In a mortar or with a nut grinder, mix them with the spices and salt.

8. Melt the butter carefully in a saucepan.

**TO SERVE:**

9. Slice the breads in half, and spread each section with browned whipped butter and artichoke dip. Or, dip the pieces of bread in melted butter followed by the herb mixture, fixing the mixture onto the bread with the butter.

## 47. Blood Orange & Pomegranate Sorbet

You'll need an ice cream machine to make these sorbets. Borrow your neighbor's if you don't have one, because it's well worth it! According to some, adding egg white to a sorbet is considered cheating, but I think it's a valid shortcut to achieve a smooth and light sorbet. You'll find pomegranate juice in your grocery store's health-food aisle.

SERVES 4–6

*⅓ vanilla bean*
*½ cup (1 dl) water*
*¾ cup (2 dl) superfine granulated sugar*
*4–6 pomegranates*
*2 cups (4½ dl) pomegranate juice, freshly squeezed*
*1 cup (2½ dl) blood orange juice, freshly squeezed*
*1 egg white, lightly whisked*
*pomegranate seeds, for garnish*

DIRECTIONS:

1. Slit the vanilla bean open lengthwise and scrape the seeds into a saucepan. Bring water, sugar, vanilla seeds, and bean pods to a boil and let the sugar dissolve. Set aside and let cool.
2. Squeeze the juice from 3 to 4 pomegranates (use the rest for garnish).
3. Mix the sugar/vanilla syrup with juices and egg white. Pour the mixture into an ice cream maker and run the machine until the sorbet is frozen and smooth.
4. Cut lids and de-seed the pomegranates, or cut the pomegranates in half to get several halves. You'll prevent messy splashes if you keep the pomegranate submerged in a bowl of water while removing the seeds.
5. Fill the hollowed-out pomegranate halves with sorbet and place them in the freezer. When serving, garnish the halves with pomegranate seeds (leftovers can be frozen or sprinkled over a salad).

## 48. Lemon Yogurt Sorbet

When I was a kid, you could buy hollowed-out lemons filled with lemon ice cream from the ice cream truck. Back then, lemon was already my favorite thing to eat. This is the first time I'm attempting to re-create this ice cream. Remember to remove the filled lemon peels from the freezer a good while before serving so they're not too hard.

SERVES 4–6

*4–6 lemons, hollowed out and with a nicely cut lid*
*1¼ cups (2½ dl) water*
*1¼ cups (2½ dl) superfine granulated sugar*
*1 tbsp food-grade glucose*
*1¼ cup (3 dl) lemon juice, freshly squeezed, plus grated peel from 2 lemons*
*1¾ cups (4 dl) Greek yogurt (10% fat)*
*3 tbsp fruity olive oil*

DIRECTIONS:

1. In a pan, bring water, sugar, glucose, and lemon peel to a boil. Let the sugar dissolve. Set aside to cool.
2. Add the lemon juice, yogurt, and olive oil to the syrup and mix well with a balloon whisk. Pour the mixture into an ice cream maker and run the machine until the sorbet is frozen and smooth.
3. Fill the hollowed-out lemon peels with the sorbet and secure the lids on top. Leave in the freezer until time to serve.

**FREEZE THE HOLLOWED-OUT SHELLS**
*Keep the hollowed out pomegranates and lemons in the freezer to prevent the sorbet from melting quickly when you want to fill them.*

**WHAT TO DRINK**
A partially sparkling Moscato wine from Italy works great here.

48.

47.

# 49. Vanilla Ice Cream Bars with Almond Crumble and Caramel Sauce

*Offer this dessert to your worst enemy, and you may just make a friend for life!*

SERVES 4–6

*1¼ lb. (500 g) chocolate chip cookies*
*5¼ oz. (150 g) almond flour*
*4½ oz. (125 g) butter, melted*
*2 pinches sea salt*
*4 cups (2 liters/20 dl) vanilla ice cream*
*1¾ cups (4 dl/1 jar caramel sauce) dulce de leche*

DIRECTIONS:

1. Line an 11¾ x 7–inch (30 x 18–cm) baking pan with parchment paper.
2. Crumble the cookies and, using your fingertips, combine them with almond flour, melted butter, and salt until the mix looks like crumbs. Press half of the crumbs into the bottom of the pan and place the pan in the freezer for 15 minutes.
3. Remove the pan from the freezer and spread the ice cream over the crumb base. Smooth out the surface with a palette knife or a spatula. Place the pan in the freezer for at least 30 to 45 minutes to give the ice cream enough time to set.
4. In a saucepan, carefully heat the caramel sauce until it is soft enough to pour. Remove the baking pan from the freezer, and drizzle the caramel sauce over the ice cream.
5. Cover the ice cream and caramel sauce with the remaining crumbs, and put the pan back in the freezer for at least another 3 hours.
6. Cut the ice cream into bars, and maybe wrap them in nice parchment paper before serving. Of course, the bars will be just as lovely if served simply on dessert plates.

## MAKE YOUR OWN CARAMEL SAUCE

*Dulce de leche can be purchased in jars, but if you'd rather make your own, here's how to do it: Place a can of sweetened, condensed milk in a large saucepan. Cover the can with water. Bring the water to a boil, and let simmer for 2 hours. It is critical that the can remains submerged in water throughout the entire cooking time, so add more water as needed. Let the can cool down a little before opening it.*

# 50. Trifle with Rum-Soaked Cherries and Biscotti

*Jars of cherries preserved in alcohol can be found at most well-stocked grocery stores today. Presto! Paired with some cream cheese and yogurt, you have dessert!*

**SERVES 4**

*½ vanilla bean*
*1½ tbsp raw cane sugar*
*½ lb. (250 g) mascarpone cream cheese*
*¾ cup (2 dl) Greek yogurt (10% fat)*
*¼ cup (½ dl) cherry juice from the jar*
*5 biscotti*
*1 jar (approx. 12¾ oz./360 g) alcohol-preserved cherries*

**DIRECTIONS:**

1. Split the vanilla bean open lengthwise and scrape out the seeds onto a cutting board. Mash the seeds with the cane sugar by pressing the side of a knife against sugar and vanilla seeds.

2. Stir the mascarpone and yogurt together thoroughly, and add in the vanilla sugar. Flavor with some of the cherry liquid and stir to a smooth cream.

3. Crush the biscotti in a mortar.

4. Layer vanilla cream, cherries, and biscotti crumbs in small cups or glasses. Chill in the refrigerator for about 15 to 20 minutes before serving.

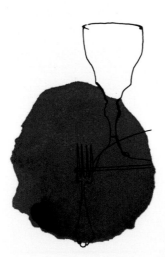

**WHAT TO DRINK**
If you haven't tried the Italian wine Recioto yet, make sure to do it with this dessert—it may be pricey, but so delicious!

# 51. Grapes in Puff Pastry with Brandy Whipped Cream

*You'll need an 8-inch-wide ovenproof cast-iron skillet to make this, as the entire pan of goodness goes in the oven when it's time to bake.*

**SERVES 4**

*4 sheets frozen puff pastry*
*¾ cup (1½ dl) superfine granulated sugar*
*2 cups (½ liter/5 dl) red seedless grapes*
*1 tbsp potato flour*
*1 oz. (25 g) butter*
*3 tbsp superfine granulated sugar*
**BRANDY WHIPPED CREAM:**
*¾ cup (2 dl) whipping cream*
*1 tbsp brandy*

**DIRECTIONS:**

1. Preheat the oven to 480°F (250°C).
2. Place the sheets of puff pastry together, two by two, sprinkling sugar between the layers. Sprinkle some sugar on the baking surface, too. When rolling out the pastry, make sure the sugar goes between the sheets of pastry as well as on the outside. Place all the pastry layers together and roll them out into one large single piece. Cut out a pastry round large enough to cover the skillet. Place the round on a piece of parchment paper.
3. Roll the grapes in potato flour to coat.
4. Heat the butter with 3 tablespoons of sugar in the cast-iron skillet until the sugar becomes a light brown caramel. Remove the skillet from the heat and add the grapes. Stir the grapes carefully to make sure they are coated with caramel.
5. Cover the skillet with the round of pastry, place the skillet into the oven, and bake for about 15 minutes, or until the pastry is puffy and the sugar on top has caramelized.
6. Whip the cream until soft peaks form and spike it with brandy.
7. Serve the dessert with a dollop of brandy cream.

**WHAT TO DRINK**
A tawny Port or a medium sweet Sherry is heavenly with the grapes.

# Sunday

*I love Sundays!*
Isn't it wonderful to wake up on Sunday morning and know there is still a whole day ahead before the next week begins? It's a whole day in which you're free to eat delicious food and spend time with family and friends. Why not invite them over for an early brunch? And for those of you feeling the after-effects of revelry the night before, these recipes will put you back on your feet!

57.

56.

53.

55.

52.

54.

# Brunch

*Sure, making brunch requires a bit of planning and shopping, but it's really worth making the effort. It's one of the nicest ways for people to get together, since it's uncomplicated and casual. Also, once it's over and your guests have gone home, there's still a good chunk of the day left for you to enjoy.*

## 52. Broccoli Fritters

A warm and savory broccoli fritter is just the ticket for Sunday brunch.

SERVES 4

   2 eggs
   ¼ cup (½ dl) all-purpose flour
   ½ cup (1 dl) Parmesan, grated
   5¼ oz. (150 g) broccoli, cooked
   butter, for frying

DIRECTIONS:

1. Mix together the eggs, flour, and Parmesan.
2. Chop the broccoli coarsely and add it to the egg/cheese batter. Shape into small burgers.
3. Sauté the burgers in butter until they're nicely browned. Serve immediately.

## 53. Baked Feta with Sage and Roasted Bell Pepper

This is a dish that's simple to make ahead. Keep the foil packets refrigerated until it's time to reheat them.

SERVES 4

   2 packages (each 5¼ oz./150 g) feta cheese
   2 garlic cloves
   2 salad onions
   2–3 canned, roasted, pointy bell peppers
   2–3 sprigs fresh sage
   black pepper, freshly ground
   2–3 tbsp olive oil

DIRECTIONS:

1. Preheat the oven to 350°F (175°C).
2. Peel and slice the garlic cloves. Thinly slice the onion and cut the bell peppers into chunks.
3. Place the cheese on two sheets of aluminum foil. Spread garlic, onion, bell pepper, and sage over each block of cheese. Season with black pepper and a few drops of olive oil. Fold the foil into small packets and heat them in the oven for 10 to 15 minutes.
4. Open the packets and serve the cheese warm, with some nice bread on the side to mop up the sauce.

## 54. Grilled Cucumber with Mozzarella and Olives

A warm cucumber infused with flavor is much tastier than a cold one. Trust me!

SERVES 4

  *1 English (hothouse) cucumber*
  *salt*
  *1–2 tbsp olive oil*
  *½ cup (1 dl) pitted kalamata olives*
  *1 package (approx. 5¼ oz./150 g) mozzarella balls*
  *1 bunch Italian parsley, leaves only*
  *½ lemon, grated peel and juice*

DIRECTIONS:

1. Peel and cut the cucumber in half. Remove seeds and then cut the cucumber into four pieces.
2. Heat a grill pan on the stovetop, or fire up the grill outside. Lightly salt the cucumber and drizzle with olive oil.
3. Grill the cucumber, de-seeded side down, for a few minutes until it is warm; turn it and put the olives, mozzarella, parsley, lemon peel, and juice into the de-seeded, hollow wedge of the cucumber. Grill over medium heat until the cheese and olives are heated through.
4. Transfer to a platter and serve the cucumber warm.

## 55. Caramelized Grapefruit with Mint

This sweet grapefruit dessert has followed me since my days on Swedish television.

SERVES 4

  *2 grapefruits*
  *4 tbsp brown sugar*
  *1½ tbsp butter*
  *1 tbsp chopped mint plus a few sprigs for garnish*

DIRECTIONS:

1. Clean and cut the grapefruits in half.
2. In a skillet, melt the butter until it is golden brown. Stir in the sugar.
3. Cook the grapefruit halves cut-side down for a few minutes in the butter/sugar mixture, until the fruit has caramelized and releases some of its juice.
4. Sprinkle with mint, and turn over the grapefruit halves in the pan to make the juice mix thoroughly with the mint.
5. Transfer the grapefruit to a platter and serve warm or lukewarm. Be careful, the sauce might be hot!

# 56. Luxury Yoggi with Granola

This is luscious enough to pass for dessert, too.

SERVES 4

GRANOLA:

*1½ cup (3 dl) rolled oats*
*½ cup (1 dl) buckwheat, crushed*
*¾ cup (1½ dl) grated coconut*
*¾ cup (2 dl) puffed rice*
*¼ cup (½ dl) sesame seeds*
*½ cup (1 dl) apple juice*
*3 tbsp light corn syrup*
*2 tbsp oil*

YOGGI:

*¾ cup (2 dl) whipping cream*
*1½ cup (3 dl) Greek yogurt (10% fat)*
*2 tsp ground cinnamon*
*4½ oz. (125 g) raspberries, strawberries, or blueberries, defrosted or fresh*
*honey (optional)*

DIRECTIONS:

1. Preheat the oven to 355°F (180°C). Place all dry ingredients for the granola on a baking sheet lined with parchment paper.
2. Mix the apple juice, corn syrup, and oil. Pour it over the grains and mix them with your fingertips until you have a moist and lumpy mix.
3. Bake the granola in the oven for about 25 minutes, or until it is nicely golden brown. Don't worry—it doesn't matter if a small lump is still a bit wet, it will dry out eventually.
4. Store the granola in a jar with a lid, and serve it for brunch or for an especially nice breakfast treat.
5. For the Yoggi, whip the cream until soft peaks form. Mix the cream, yogurt, and cinnamon, and fold in the berries. Set aside. If you wish, sweeten it with some honey. Personally, I think it's sweet enough with just the granola.

# 57. Baked Pears with Garlic and Coppa Ham

It's important to use soft pears for this recipe—not the Anjou variety.

SERVES 4

*5 soft pears*
*2¾ oz. (75 g) unsalted butter*
*1 tbsp brown sugar*
*1 red chili*
*1 whole head garlic*
*½ lemon, juice*
*8–10 slices Coppa ham*

DIRECTIONS:

1. Peel the pears and cut them in half, as shown on page 102. Place the pear halves in a high-sided baking dish. Melt the butter and brown sugar in a saucepan.
2. Chop the chili and mix it with the butter. Pour the butter/sugar/chili mixture over the pears. Cut the garlic in half, straight across the middle, and add that in the dish. Cover the dish with foil and bake in the oven for 30 minutes. Remove the foil during the last 10 minutes to let the pears develop some color—the juicier they are, the better.
3. Squeeze some lemon juice over the dish, and serve with slices of Coppa.

*Yes, please! A luxury yoggi with granola!*

58.

59.

# The Hangover Brunch

*Hangovers happen to us all at some point, right? For me, waking up with a hangover means I've had a great time the evening before, in which I've met lots of nice people, danced the night away, and gone to bed way too late! A weekend cookbook would not be complete without a few hangover recipes, so here's one for huevos rancheros, accompanied by an ice-cold Bloody Raspberry.*

## 58. Huevos Rancheros with Spicy Sausage and Jalapeño

A classic Mexican egg dish served at breakfast: it's eggs the rancher's way! By all means, turn this meal into individual dishes; not only does it look good, it's also nice to get your very own dish.

SERVES 4

*1 shallot*
*2 fresh jalapeños*
*2 spicy sausages or Mexican chorizo*
*2 tomatoes*
*1 can (approx. 15 oz./425 g) baby corn on the cobs*
*1 can (approx. 14 oz./400 g) black beans, cooked*
*3 tbsp olive oil*
*salt*
*black pepper, freshly ground*
*4 corn tortillas*
*4 large eggs*
*1 lime*
*1 bunch fresh cilantro, chopped*

DIRECTIONS:

1. Preheat the oven to 350°F (175°C).
2. Peel and finely chop the shallot. Thinly slice the jalapeños and sausages, and coarsely chop tomatoes and baby corn on the cobs.
3. Heat olive oil in a skillet and quickly sauté the onion, jalapeños, tomatoes, corn, beans, and sausages for a few minutes over high heat. Season with salt and pepper. Transfer to a platter.
4. Fry a tortilla in some olive oil in the skillet. Turn the tortilla after 1 to 2 minutes.
5. Spread vegetables and sausages over the tortilla, and break a raw egg on top. Place the skillet in the oven and bake until the egg is set, about 5 to 8 minutes depending on how runny you like your egg. Do the same with the rest of the tortillas.
6. Squeeze lime juice over dish, and sprinkle with some chopped cilantro when serving.

## 59. Grilled Pancetta Egg

Why not enjoy these tasty eggs with some Parmesan bread? (See page 57.)

SERVES 4

*2 tomatoes on the vine*
*1 bunch chives*
*4–8 slices pancetta*
*4 large eggs*
*salt*
*black pepper, freshly ground*
*3 tbsp whipping cream*
*4 tbsp aged cheese, grated*

DIRECTIONS:

1. Preheat the oven to 390°F (200°C) and turn on the broiler.
2. Finely dice the tomatoes, and chop the chives. Spread tomatoes and chives over the bottom of four ovenproof individual dishes.
3. Place a few slices of pancetta in each dish, and break an egg over them. Season with salt and pepper.
4. Drizzle with some cream and top with grated cheese. Place the dishes in the oven and bake for 5 to 7 minutes, or until the surface is lightly golden and the egg looks set.

## 60. Bloody Raspberry

If your head isn't pounding too badly, feel free to swap the lemonade for some Prosecco.

SERVES 4

*1¼ cups (2½ dl) raspberries*
*1¾ cups (4 dl) club soda*
*1 tbsp confectioner's sugar*
*½ cup (1 dl) lemonade*
*4–6 ice cubes*

DIRECTIONS:

1. Mix everything together in a blender or food processor.
2. Pour into a glass, and make sure to top it off with some extra Prosecco at the table.

## 61. Grilled Smoked Ham with Mustard Red Cabbage and Egg Yolk

If your headache hasn't subsided after this meal, well, you may as well go back to bed.

SERVES 4

> 1 small can (approx. ¾ cup/2 dl) chopped red cabbage
> 1 tbsp coarse-grained sweet mustard
> ½ tbsp white wine vinegar
> 4 slices (approx. 10½ oz./300 g) smoked ham
> 4 large egg yolks

DIRECTIONS:

1. Heat the red cabbage, and season with mustard and vinegar.
2. Cook the smoked ham in a grill pan.
3. Place the slices of ham on a plate and top with red cabbage. Make a hole in the cabbage and drop an egg yolk into it. Top with mustard.

## 62. Mango & Banana Drink with Coconut

If you prefer a thicker beverage, use vanilla ice cream instead of milk.

SERVES 4

> 7 oz. (200 g) frozen mango
> 1 banana
> ¾ cup (2 dl) coconut milk
> ½ cup (1 dl) milk
> ¾ cup (2 dl) ice cubes
> juice of 1 lemon

DIRECTIONS:

1. Place all ingredients in a pitcher, and mix with an immersion blender.
2. Pour into glasses and serve immediately.

## 63. Sautéed Hot-Smoked Pork Belly with Buttered Peas and Soy Beans

Simple is tasty!

SERVES 4

> 14 oz.–1 lb. (400–500 g) smoked pork belly
> 1 small yellow onion
> ¾ cup (2 dl) green peas
> ¾ cup (2 dl) green soybeans (edamame)
> 2½ oz. (¾ dl) water
> 3–4 tbsp butter
> 2 tbsp lemon juice, freshly squeezed
> salt
> black pepper, freshly ground

DIRECTIONS:

1. Cut the pork belly into thick slices. Peel and chop the onion fine. In a large and deep skillet, brown both sides of the pork slices in butter. Season with salt and pepper and transfer to a plate.
2. In the same pan, cook the onion in butter until soft. Add in peas, beans, and water. Let the water cook off, and add the rest of the butter toward the end to make thin, buttery gravy in the pan.
3. Return the pork slices to the skillet and season with lemon juice, salt, and freshly ground black pepper.
4. Serve immediately while everything is warm.

61.

62.

63.

# 64. French Toast (Swedish Poor Knights) with Asparagus, Shrimp, and Hollandaise Sauce

*This is closer to French Toast than Swedish Poor Knights, since it's paired with both asparagus and shrimp!*

## SERVES 4

**FRENCH TOAST (POOR KNIGHTS):**
2 large eggs
¼ cup (½ dl) whipping cream
¼ cup (½ dl) milk
1 pinch salt
4 thick slices sourdough bread
butter, for frying

**HOLLANDAISE SAUCE:**
1 shallot
7 oz. (200 g) butter
3 tbsp water
3 tbsp lemon juice, freshly squeezed
3 large egg yolks
salt
white pepper, freshly ground
Worcestershire sauce, to taste

**SIDES:**
1 bunch green or white asparagus
1–1½ lbs. (500–600 g) cooked shrimp, unpeeled

## DIRECTIONS:

1. Lightly whisk eggs, cream, and milk together. Season with salt. Dredge and turn the slices of bread in the batter to let them soak up some of the batter.
2. In a skillet, cook the French toast on both sides in butter. Keep warm.

### SIDES:

3. Cook the asparagus until al dente, 2 to 3 minutes, in lightly salted water. Keep the asparagus warm.
4. Peel the shrimp and set them aside.

### HOLLANDAISE SAUCE:

5. Peel and finely chop the shallot. Melt the butter.
6. Bring water, lemon juice, and shallot to boil in a saucepan and let the liquid boil until it is reduced and only half remains. Remove saucepan from heat. Whisk in the egg yolks and continue whisking over very low heat or over a water bath until you have a fluffy sauce.
7. Add the warm butter, one drop at a time, while stirring. The sauce must have a temperature of 113°F to 122°F (45°C to 50°C). Whisk until the sauce has thickened. Season with salt and freshly ground white pepper and a few drops of Worcestershire sauce.

### TO SERVE:

8. Transfer the warm French toast onto plates. Place the asparagus and shrimp on top, and drizzle with Hollandaise sauce. Enjoy immediately.

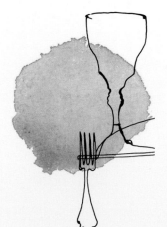

## WHAT TO DRINK

The top choice for this dish is vintage Champagne with notes of toast and ripe apples. An excellent and budget-friendly option is a Cremant d'Alsace, but even a dry white wine from the Loire Valley, made from the Chenin Blanc grape, would be good here.

# 65. Green Sandwich Layer Cake with Hot-Smoked Salmon and Avocado

*The very best sandwich layer cake is one that is made in advance and has had time to rest, preferably overnight. If made ahead, delay decorating it until right before serving.*

MAKES 8–10 SLICES

*1 loaf (approx. 1¼ lb./520 g) sandwich bread*
*1 avocado*
*10 small blemish-free tomatoes*
SALMON FILLING:
*1½ lbs. (700 g) hot-smoked salmon, reserve 3½ oz. (100 g) for garnish*
*4 tbsp mayonnaise*
EGG FILLING:
*8 large eggs, boiled*
*2 containers (each approx. 1 oz./30 g) chives*
*2 tbsp Dijon mustard*
GREEN FROSTING:
*2 avocados*
*10½ oz. (300 g) green peas, cooked*
*2 tsp salt*
*Tabasco sauce, to taste*

DIRECTIONS:

FILLINGS:

1. Mash the salmon for the salmon filling with a fork until chunky. Reserve 3½ oz. (100 g) for garnish. Mix it with the mayonnaise.

2. Chop the eggs and chives for the egg filling and set some aside for garnish. Mix with the mustard.

3. Cover a large tray with plastic wrap, and place a few slices of bread onto it. Spread all the salmon filling onto the slices. Add another layer of bread slices, and spread the egg filling over this layer. Add the last layer of bread and press down gently. Cover the cakes with plastic wrap and refrigerate.

GREEN FROSTING:

4. Cut one of the avocados in half; remove the pit, and scoop out the flesh. In a food processor or with an immersion blender, mix avocado and peas to a smooth purée. Season with salt and Tabasco sauce.

TO SERVE:

5. Remove the cakes from the refrigerator. Cut the remaining avocado in half and remove the pit. Scoop out the flesh and cut it into wedges. Cut the tomatoes into thin slices. Spread the green frosting over the cake. Garnish with salmon, avocado wedges, chives, and thin tomato slices.

**WHAT TO DRINK**

The best wines to go with this sandwich layer cake would be a Pinot Gris from Alsace or a young Riesling from Austria.

67.

66.

# 66. Almond Tartlets with Lemon Posset and Berries

The original lemon posset was an English beverage dating back to the Middle Ages. Today it is the name given to a fresh lemon crème.

MAKES APPROX. 12 TARTLETS
4½ oz. (125 g) almond paste
5¼ oz. (150 g) cold butter (straight from the refrigerator), in pieces
1¾ cups (4 dl) all-purpose flour
1 large egg
1/5 tsp salt

LEMON POSSET:
2½ cups (3 dl) heavy whipping cream
½ cup (1 dl) superfine granulated sugar
1 lemon, grated peel plus ¼ cup juice

TO SERVE:
fresh berries such as blackberries or red currants

DIRECTIONS:
1. Preheat the oven to 390°F (200°C).
2. In a food processor or by hand, mix almond paste, butter, flour, egg, and salt to make pliable dough.
3. Line 12 individual oval-shaped cookie tins, or mini-tartlet tins, with the dough, pressing to spread it thin. Let the tins sit in the freezer for about 30 minutes.
4. Place the cold, lined cookie tins onto a cookie sheet and bake them on the oven's middle rack for about 15 minutes. Remove from the oven and let cool.
5. In a saucepan, bring the cream and sugar for the lemon posset to a boil. Continue cooking while stirring continuously for another 3 minutes. Remove the saucepan from the heat and add in the lemon juice. Let the crème cool a little.
6. Stir in the finely grated lemon peel, and whisk vigorously until the crème thickens. Pour into a dish or bowl and refrigerate overnight so it sets completely.
7. Fill almond tartlets with the lemon posset and top with fresh berries.

# 67. Cinnamon & Cardamom Sticks

I became completely obsessed with ready-to-use pizza dough for a while. Here is the end result!

MAKES 25–30 STICKS
¾ cup (2 dl) superfine granulated sugar
½ cup (1 dl) brown sugar
1 tsp ground cardamom
2 tsp ground cinnamon
1 roll of ready-to-use pizza dough
melted butter

DIRECTIONS:
1. Preheat the oven to 390°F (200°C).
2. Mix sugars and spices together. With a rolling pin, press the spiced sugar into the dough, saving a few tablespoons to sprinkle over the sticks.
3. Cut the dough into thin strips and twist them at each end. Place the sticks onto a baking sheet lined with parchment paper and brush them with melted butter. Sprinkle with the reserved spicy sugar.
4. Bake the sticks for 10 to 12 minutes. Let them cool on a rack.

# 68. Marie José's Chocolate Cake

*This cake, dating from my time at the restaurant Petri Pumpa in Lund, Sweden, was a staple on the bar's menu. It is by far the best chocolate cake I have ever eaten! I filched the recipe for it, so now you can enjoy this cake, too.*

MAKES ABOUT 12 SERVINGS

*10½ oz. (300 g) dark chocolate (70% cacao is preferred)*
*10½ oz. (300 g) unsalted butter*
*7 large eggs*
*10½ oz. (approx. 1⅝ cups/3¼ dl) superfine granulated sugar*
*½ cup (1 dl) all-purpose flour*

TO SERVE:

*confectioner's sugar*
*fresh berries such as strawberries or raspberries*
*lightly whipped cream*

DIRECTIONS:

1. Preheat the oven to 350°F (175°C).
2. Butter a springform cake pan and dust it with sugar.
3. Melt chocolate and butter together in a bowl over a hot water bath.
4. Separate the eggs into yolks and whites. With an electric mixer, beat the yolks and sugar until light and voluminous. Sift in the flour. In another bowl, beat the egg whites until stiff peaks form.
5. Fold the chocolate butter into the egg yolk batter, and mix thoroughly. Carefully fold in the egg whites, and then pour the batter into the springform pan.
6. Bake the cake for 45 to 50 minutes (it will still be slightly gooey at the center). It's important not to overbake this cake, so remove it from the oven a little bit early to be on the safe side. Let the cake cool completely in the springform pan.
7. Dust the cake with confectioner's sugar and serve it with fresh berries and lightly whipped cream.

**WHAT TO DRINK**

Chocolate + rum = a match made in heaven! Why not give some craft rum from the West Indies a try? It's intensely fruity and flavorful.

# 69. "Upside-Down" Apple Cake

*Sometimes you just have to do things a different way, so why not turn an apple cake upside down?*

MAKES 8–10 SERVINGS

¾ cup (2 dl) dark brown sugar
2¾ oz. (75 g) butter
1 tsp salt
5–7 medium Golden Delicious apples

CAKE BATTER:

9 oz. (250 g) unsalted butter
½ cup (1 dl) brown sugar
½ cup (1 dl) superfine granulated sugar
4 large eggs
1¼ cup (3 dl) all-purpose flour
3 tsp baking powder
¼ cup (½ dl) brandy
2 tsp ground cardamom

RAW CUSTARD:

3 large egg yolks
¼ cup (½ dl) superfine granulated sugar
½ tsp vanilla sugar
1 cup (2½ dl) whipped cream

DIRECTIONS:

1. Preheat the oven to 390°F (200°C).
2. In a saucepan, warm the brown sugar, butter, and salt, and whisk them together to make an evenly thick sauce.
3. Cut the apples into thick wedges, leaving the skin on. Grease the sides of a 9½-inch-wide springform pan with butter and coat with sugar; line the bottom of the pan with a piece of parchment paper.
4. Cover the bottom of the springform pan with the brown sugar sauce, and arrange the apple wedges attractively on top.
5. Beat the butter and sugar until light and airy for the cake batter. Add in the eggs, one a time, whisking between additions, and add the rest of the ingredients to make a thick, smooth batter. Flavor with brandy.
6. Bake the cake on the middle rack of the oven for 45 minutes, or until golden brown and firm. Turn the pan upside down and remove the cake so that the apples at the bottom of the cake are facing up.
7. Beat yolks, sugar, and vanilla sugar to make raw custard. Fold in the whipped cream.
8. Serve the cake with raw custard on the side.

**WHAT TO DRINK**
Serve a fine Tokayer or a Moscatel de Setúbal with this luscious apple dessert.

# INDEX

Skyhorse Publishing books may be purchased in bulk at special discounts for sales promotion, corporate gifts, fund-raising, or educational purposes. Special editions can also be created to specifications. For details, contact the Special Sales Department, Skyhorse Publishing, 307 West 36th Street, 11th Floor, New York, NY 10018 or info@skyhorsepublishing.com.

Skyhorse® and Skyhorse Publishing® are registered trademarks of Skyhorse Publishing, Inc.®, a Delaware corporation.
Visit our website at www.skyhorsepublishing.com.

10 9 8 7 6 5 4 3 2 1

Library of Congress Cataloging-in-Publication Data is available on file.

*Photographer*: Charlie Drevstam, assistant Louise Martinsson
*Illustrator*: Stina Wirsén
*Graphics*: Annika Lyth
*Recipe development*: Benny Cederberg
*Drink suggestions*: Stefan Petersson/Giertz Wine Imports
*Swedish Editor:* Anna Paljak
*Repro*: Elanders, Värnamo
*Swedish Printer for original Swedish edition:* Livonia Print, Latvia 2014

Print ISBN: 978-1-5107-0967-6
Ebook ISBN: 978-1-5107-0973-7

Printed in China